1 Corinthians

Baker Bible Guides

General Editors:
Ian Coffey and Stephen Gaukroger

Old Testament Editor: Stephen Dray
New Testament Editor: Stephen Motyer

Isaiah: Philip Hacking
Mark: David Hewitt
Acts: Stephen Gaukroger
Ephesians: Stephen Motyer
Philippians: Ian Coffey
Timothy & Titus: Michael Griffiths
1 Peter: Andrew Whitman

1 Corinthians

Free to Grow

Robin Dowling
and Stephen Dray

BakerBooks

A Division of Baker Book House Co.
Grand Rapids, Michigan 49516

© 1995 by Robin Dowling and Stephen Dray

Published by Baker Books
a division of Baker Book House Company
P.O. Box 6287, Grand Rapids, MI 49516-6287

First American edition, 1996

Printed in the United States of America

First published in 1995 by Crossway Books
Leicester, England

Library of Congress Cataloging-in-Publication Data

Dowling, Robin, 1946–
    1 Corinthians : free to grow / Robin Dowling and Stephen Dray. — 1st American ed.
        p.   cm. — (Baker Bible guides)
    Originally published: Leicester, England : Crossway Books, 1995.
    Includes bibliographical references.
    ISBN 0-8010-5724-8 (pbk.)
    1. Bible. N.T. Corinthians, 1st—Criticism, interpretation, etc. 2. Bible. N.T. Corinthians, 1st—Study and teaching. I. Dray, Stephen, 1951– . II. Title. III. Series.
BS2675.2.D68 1996
227'.207—dc20   96-46091

For information about academic books, resources for Christian leaders, and all new releases available from Baker Book House, visit our web site:
http://www.bakerbooks.com

To
our wives and children

Clara
Timothy, Anne, Martin, Lydia,
Peter and Abigail Dowling

Anne
Peter, John and Anna Dray

Contents

Contents

Baker Bible Guides

Series Editors' Introduction

Meeting together in groups to study the Bible appears to be a booming leisure-time activity in many parts of the world. This series has been designed to help such groups and, in particular, those who lead them.

We are also aware of the needs of those who preach and teach to larger groups as well as the hard-pressed student, all of whom often look for a commentary that gives a concise summary and lively application of a particular passage.

We have tried to keep three clear aims in our sights:

1 To explain and apply the message of the Bible in non-technical language.

2 To encourage discussion, prayer and action on what the Bible teaches.

3 To enlist authors who are in the business of teaching the Bible to others and are doing it well.

All of us engaged in the project believe that the Bible is the Word of God - given to us in order that people might discover him and his purposes for our lives. We believe that the 66 books which go to make up the Bible, although written by different people, in different places, at different times, through different circumstances, have a single unifying theme: that theme is Salvation.

All of us hope that the books in this series will help people get a grip on the message of the Bible. But most important of all, we pray that the Bible will get a grip on you as a result!

Ian Coffey
Stephen Gaukroger
Series Editors

Note to readers

In our Bible Guides we have developed special symbols to make things easier to follow. Every passage therefore has an opening section which is the passage in a nutshell.

The main section is the one that makes sense of the passage.

Questions
Every passage also has special questions for group and personal study after the main section. Some questions are addressed to us as individuals, some speak to us as members of our church or home group, while others concern us as members of God's people worldwide.

Digging deeper

Some passages, however, require an extra amount of explanation, and we have put these sections into two categories. The first kind gives additional background material that helps us to understand something complex. For example, if we dig deeper into the gospels, it helps us to know who the Pharisees were, so that we can see more easily why they related to Jesus in the way they did. These technical sections are marked with a spade.

Important doctrines

The second kind of background section appears with passages which have important doctrines contained in them, and which we need to study in more depth if we are to grow as Christians. Special sections that explain them to us in greater detail are marked with this symbol.

How to use this book

1 Corinthians is probably one of the least read books in the New Testament. Certain passages are well known (chapters 7, 12–15 and parts of chapter 11), but the book as a whole is neglected. Yet it is virtually impossible to understand what Paul is saying in this letter unless the parts are seen in the light of the whole. The result is that, where only parts are studied, it is difficult to understand even that section accurately.

This book has been designed to help you to study the whole letter in fourteen weeks. The authors of the book would recommend that this, rather than a bitty approach, is adopted if 1 Corinthians is to be used in a home group. At times this involves looking at quite large chunks of text (*e.g.* 8:1 – 11:1) but, we would suggest that the effort required will be amply rewarded.

We are aware of the particular interest that certain sections of the letter arouse today, for example, chapters 7, 12 and 14. As a result more detailed attention has been given to these passages. Such attention does not mean that we believe that these are the most important sections of the book; Paul certainly thought the issues raised earlier in the letter were far more vital. However, we do hope that the careful attention we have given to these passages will ensure that they are not misunderstood, as they so often are.

This book has been written on the assumption that it will be used in one of three ways:

- for individuals using it as an aid to personal study

- for groups wishing to use it as a study guide to 1 Corinthians

- for those preparing to teach others.

Personal study
One of the best methods of Bible study is to read the text through care-

fully several times, possibly using different versions or translations. Having reflected on the material it is a good discipline to write down your own thoughts before doing anything else. At this stage the introduction of other books can be useful. If you are using this book as your main study resource, then read through the relevant sections carefully, turning up the Bible references that are mentioned. Verse references are in parentheses (*e.g.* (1) refers to verse 1). The questions at the end of each chapter are specifically designed to help you to apply the passage to your own situation. You may find it helpful to write your answers to the questions in your notes.

It is a good habit to conclude with prayer, bringing before God the things you have learned.

Group study

Members of the group should follow the guidelines set out above for 'Personal study'. It is recommended that your own notes should contain:

a. Questions or comments on verses that you wish to discuss with the whole group.
b. Answers to the questions at the end of each section.

The format of your group time will depend on your leader, but it is suggested that the answers to the questions at the end of each section form a starting point for your discussions.

We have been enormously blessed in doing the study required to produce this book. We trust that you, too, will be helped to know God better in your study of 1 Corinthians.

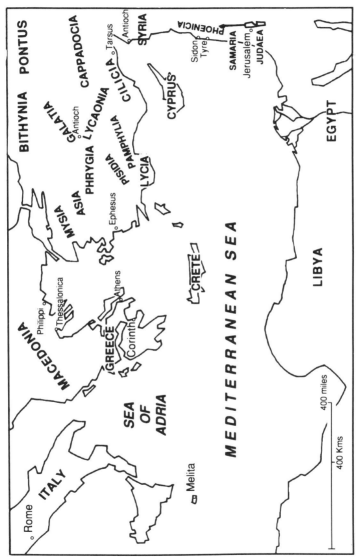

The Near East in the first century A.D., showing the central location of Corinth

WELCOME TO CORINTH!
1 Corinthians 1:1–9

1 Corinthians 1:1–3
A letter to take notice of!

Faced with a divided church, Paul uses his authority as an apostle to try and re-unite the fellowship in Corinth. His advice has a lasting value.

The background

Paul had first visited Corinth on his second missionary journey, about AD 50. This had followed a rather unsuccessful trip to Athens. He spent about eighteen months at Corinth during which he lodged with two Jewish believers, Aquila and his wife, Priscilla, who had been exiled from Rome when the emperor Claudius ordered all Jews to leave. There Paul began a programme of evangelism in the synagogue, but the Jews opposed him so he had concentrated his activities upon the rest of the population in the city: the 'Gentiles'. His base was the home of a man called Titius Justus. Paul's ministry proved successful and many were converted to the Christian faith. Yet the period was not without its difficulties and on one occasion Paul had been brought before the city ruler, the proconsul Gallio. We read about this in Acts 18.

After leaving Corinth, Paul does not appear to have had much to do with the church he had founded there. However, on his third missionary journey about AD 52–55, while at Ephesus, contact was re-established. Unfortunately the news he received was not good, for the church seemed to be tolerating immorality among its members. This prompted him to write a letter to the church rebuking them (5:9) but it was misunderstood (5:10, 11). This misunderstanding had been reported back to Paul and, at the same time, he had been informed by members of the household of Chloe of further disorders (1:11). Apparently, he had also received a delegation from the church which was led by Stephanus, Fortunatus and Achaicus who had brought a letter with a number of questions upon which the church sought answers (16:17; 7:1). The result of this was 1 Corinthians, a letter which gives us a more intimate glimpse into one of the early churches than any of the other New Testament writings.

Just as today there is a standard way in addressing a letter, so there was in Paul's time. Verses 1–3 follow that pattern by giving the name of the senders (1), the addressees (2) and offering a brief greeting (3).

These early verses reflect both Paul's problems with the Corinthian congregation and, also, indicate the high hopes he had for them. We see this immediately with his appeal to his apostleship.

What is an apostle?

The word apostle is used in a variety of ways in the New Testament. Sometimes it refers to missionaries and at other times it is used of church messengers. But supremely it is used of those whom Jesus entrusted with the teaching of authentic Christianity. In this sense it is only ever used of the eleven disciples of Jesus and of Paul himself (and of Matthias in Acts 1:26). This is how Paul uses the word here.

This is important, for among the Corinthians were those who claimed special authority in the church and were twisting the gospel message. Paul insists upon his own authority. In doing this he reminds his readers of his unique call by God. They would have all been familiar with his testimony (see Acts 9, especially verse 15) as the missionary and founder of Christianity in the non-Jewish world. He also reminds them that the whole of his ministry is determined by the will of God. Thus he rebukes those who would set themselves up over and against the calling and will of the Lord Jesus.

Two thousand years later we live in days long after the deaths of all the early founders of Christianity. Yet we still have their ministry, for what they taught was written down and has been preserved in the writings of the New Testament. Thus, wherever those writings are read and faithfully explained, the apostolic ministry is found today. It is up to us to uphold and apply all that they taught!

Paul was not alone in addressing the Corinthians, for Sosthenes joined in greeting them. A Sosthenes is mentioned in Acts 18:17. He was a ruler of the Corinthian synagogue who was beaten before Gallio because he sympathized with Paul. It is tempting to assume that this same man was now Paul's assistant in Ephesus, especially since Sosthenes was not a very common name in those days, but, we cannot be sure. What is more important to us is his description as *our brother*. This was the characteristic way in which the early Christians addressed one another. It was not a mere formality. The distinctions which divided men and women and alienated them from one another were to have no place among them. From what we shall later learn of the Corinthian church the use of the word 'brother' here was a necessary (if gentle) reminder, because they were divided themselves. We also need to remember this fundamental teaching in our twentieth-century fellowships of Jesus.

Questions

1. What importance do I place upon Bible Study? In what ways might Paul's words here challenge me to greater effort?
2. God expects his churches to be family fellowships. Is this true of our church and, if not, why not?
3. Non-Christians should notice that the church is different from the society in which they live. What sort of differences should they see?

1 Corinthians 1:1–3 (concluded)
King Jesus and his fellow citizens

Christian churches are expected to be united fellowships of holy people who follow the lead of King Jesus.

 Paul's next words probably also carry a rebuke. For Paul does not write to the 'Corinthian Church' but *the church of God in Corinth*. How tempting it is to think of 'our church'. But this is not what the Bible teaches. Each individual fellowship of believers is both a small copy and a part of the universal church which has but one leader! The Corinthians had forgotten this and had divided into parties and cared little for the churches of God elsewhere. The apostle gently rebukes their folly and ours. We should surely think far less of what divides us and far more of the gospel which unites us. What a blessing that would be!

Not that Paul would tolerate the flabby teaching which today so often parades itself under the banner of unity. This is clear from his next words: *sanctified in Christ Jesus*. 'Sanctified' means to be set apart by the offering of sacrifice. The Christian is a person who knows that he or she has been set apart for God because of the sacrifice Jesus made for sin upon the cross. This is the basis of our unity, not the acceptance of everybody's ideas whether they are biblical or not.

Then Paul adds, 'called to be saints'. Those who are separated to God in Jesus are to live a life which reflects his own holiness; a lesson which the Corinthian church seemed to have long forgotten. It is a truth which we, too, very easily forget. We tend to think of 'saints' as very special Christians, set apart from run-of-the-mill believers. Yet every one of us is called to be a saint. The Bible simply will not tolerate two groups of Christians: the saints and the sloppy! Every one of us is to demonstrate that we truly are the people of God by being mirror-images of Jesus. Nothing else is acceptable to God. The final words of verse 2 emphasize this: all who serve God everywhere receive the same calling from Jesus, there are no exceptions!

Grace and peace

The early church quickly adopted two words almost as 'passwords': grace and peace. We can never fathom the depth and height of their meaning; they sum up all the treasures of the Christian message. Grace points to the completely unmerited and undeserved character of all of God's dealings with us. The Christian can never stand before God except for his mercy. He it was who loved us when we were unlovely and rebellious. He it was who became man in order to meet our need of forgiveness. He it was who gave us strength to believe and keeps us in his way. Peace describes the result of grace. It is the ending of God's hostility to us and includes every blessing that is and will one day be ours as Christians.

Each comes to us from the Father as the source and the Lord Jesus Christ as the means or agent. He it is who, by his death, has secured such grace and peace to all who believe. Hallelujah!

One of the remarkable features about these early verses is the number of times that Jesus is mentioned: ten times in ten verses! Why? The letter was not going to be an easy one to write and the people who received it were less than godly. Surely, Paul's repeated emphasis upon Jesus is intended to remind both the Corinthians (and us!) that there is only one person who can resolve the sad situations which so often develop in our churches. At the foot of the cross of Jesus we are to be melted and refashioned in his image. Perhaps we struggle because many of us have not recently been back to the place where we first met the Lord?

Finally, we note that Paul had the highest possible view of Jesus. He is to be worshipped ('called upon': verse 2), something that the Bible forbids to any except God; he is given the divine title 'Lord' three times (2, 3) and he is described as equal to the Father (3). Jesus is God: nothing less is the Christian view of Jesus of Nazareth.

How significant that Paul should make such claims in this letter! Surely he calls both the Corinthians and all who read their correspondence to recognize that there is but one Lord in the church. Every personal prejudice and ambition is to be brought to his feet. It is he alone who is to rule us. He is the king. We are to listen and follow him.

Questions
1. Am I content to be a flabby, sloppy 'Christian'? What do I need to learn from this passage?
2. How central to the ambitions of our churches is the desire for unity?
3. What implications do Paul's view of Jesus have for multi-faith activities?

1 Corinthians 1:4–9
The church God blesses!

The Corinthian church was in danger of forgetting the God who had blessed them. Paul calls them back to unite in the truth.

 In Paul's day letters between those who shared the same religious beliefs normally opened with thanksgiving which hinted at what was to come. In all Paul's letters the thanksgiving follows a similar pattern. He gives thanks • always • to God • on behalf of the Christians to whom he writes • because of the things God has done for them.

A gifted church

We can well understand Paul's unending thankfulness to God for the church at Corinth. His preaching ('the testimony of Jesus': verse 6) had reaped a rich harvest. So had that of Apollos and others who had ministered in the city. The Holy Spirit had taken the message that the Corinthians had heard and had first convinced them of its truth and then changed their lives to prove it. A large and thriving church had been established and, for all its problems, was a remarkable testimony to the grace of God.

The church was not only large but remarkably gifted (5, 7). This was especially true of their 'word-ministries' and wisdom. The Corinthians were in danger of misusing these gifts, but Paul was none the less grateful to God for the way he had so markedly granted to the church the resources they needed to attain maturity and to be preserved in their calling (7–9).

Yet one of the great failings of the Corinthian church (as with many large or gifted churches) was that many of its members considered that their giftedness reflected well on themselves, that in some way they had earned such blessings. In response, Paul reminds them that all they are and have is the result of the grace of God mediated to them in Christ Jesus. The emphasis lies on the unmerited gifts of God: he alone is the object of boasting.

From first to last the Christian is a debtor to God's grace. It was grace that first aroused the believer to seek the Lord; it was grace that gave repentance and faith; it was and is grace that equips and guides the Christian day by day. When this is grasped boasting, pride and self-seeking can have no place. We can but stand in awe and wonder and, together, marvel at the amazing grace of God.

Then the Christians at Corinth were forgetting that the Christian faith looks forward to the return of Jesus. They had become so pre-occupied with their present riches that they had neglected their hope. The purpose of God's gifting was, Paul says, to assist them to remain steadfast to the end. God was not going to let them down. Having first and graciously drawn them to faith ('called') through their fellowship with Jesus, he was not about to fail to bring his work to completion!

Encouragement for new believers

A newly converted Christian very soon finds that the way forward is full of hidden dangers and snares. It is easy to become fearful and to ask the question, 'Can I keep going as a believer?' Paul replies that this is the wrong thing to ask. Rather the question should be, 'Can I rely on God?' The answer to this is clear-cut: God is faithful and will give all the necessary resources.

But, the questioner might ask, 'How can I be sure?' Paul replies that the fact that anyone believes at all is evidence of the grace of God, and he does not go back on a work he has begun. More than that, however, the very transformation of life which results from believing the good news about Jesus is itself a tribute to the power of God which is at work. Finally, Paul points to all the resources that God has provided for his people which are designed to support and help the Christian. Such are the ground for confidence, but not in self, in God!

These resources are to be found within the church, not in individual believers on their own. God equips local fellowships with a range of abilities through the proper exercise of which the individual believers grow and come to maturity. Every Christian leader will tell you that the believers who grow are those who meet together regularly and share the ministries that God has given them to build one another up. Those who neglect to meet together invariably seem to shrivel up and deprive others of help too.

However, in a remarkable way God had established and equipped the Corinthian church. No wonder Paul begins this paragraph with the words, *I always thank God for you.*

Questions
1. Are you certain you are a Christian? What lessons can we learn here that can help us be sure?
2. How might the church we belong to be in danger of thinking well of itself?
3. The gospel had an enormous effect on pagan Corinth. What might we discover from this passage to help us to reach the ungodly world around us?

Corinthian slogans and quotations

The New Testament was written in Greek. In the first century this meant that it would have been written in capital letters and without punctuation. Usually this creates no difficulty since it is quite obvious what the original author intended to say; the agreement between different versions of the Bible shows that punctuation is rarely a significant fact in the interpretation of a passage in the New Testament.

Without punctuation, however, it is sometimes difficult to tell whether the words are the author's own or whether he is quoting from elsewhere.

In 1 Corinthians it is generally agreed that Paul not only refers to the letter that the church had sent him but sometimes quotes (not always with approval!) phrases from it. In addition, most agree that he sometimes uses their favourite slogan-words and quotes them back (again, not always with approval!).

Words like 'wisdom' and 'knowledge' were favoured slogan-words, as were 'spirituals' when referring to God's gracious gifts. Paul often uses such slogans and tries to show how the Corinthians were in error in their understanding or emphasis upon such words and the ideas that lay behind them. Other possible examples include *the deep things of God* (2:10), *everything is permissible* (6:12; 10:23) and *beyond what is written* (4:6).

Later (from chapter 7 onwards, see 7:1), Paul seems sometimes to quote from the church's letter: for example, 7:1 itself probably contains a quote: 'It is good for a man not even to touch a woman'. Controversially, some argue that 14:33b–35 is a quote and does not reflect Paul's view but that of his opponents!

Whatever opinions one adopts on the details, it seems that slogans are cited and quotations made in the letter. In a careful reading of the letter we have to be aware that this sometimes takes place.

Utterance and knowledge

It soon becomes clear that Paul is using two of the Corinthians' own 'catchwords' in verse 5. In the Greek world of Corinth both eloquence and 'spiritual' knowledge were highly regarded and zealously sought. The gifts that the church particularly cherished were word-gifts and gifts of 'understanding'. It seems, then, that Paul here recognizes that these gifts are a singular demonstration of the goodness of God to the Corinthians. Later, of course, he will have to take issue with their misuse. Here he rejoices in the fact that God has granted such gifts to them.

TRUE AND FALSE WISDOM
1 Corinthians 1:10 – 2:16

1 Corinthians 1:10–17
The danger of divisions

The Corinthian church was sadly divided. Paul expresses his great concern and shows his readers what they must do to put the matter right.

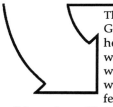 The Corinthian fellowship was something to thank God for, but it was not a perfect church! Paul had heard from some of *Chloe's household* that splits were emerging among the members (11). Chloe was probably an Ephesian merchant-woman who was well known, through trading links, with the fellowship at Corinth. Her household (slaves) may well have been Christians who met with the Corinthian church when in the city. Certainly, they knew Paul and his avid interest in the fellowship he had founded.

Now this information had not been relayed to Paul either in the letter the Corinthians had sent or by their delegation to him. Yet his reply shows that this matter was more important than everything else and so he tackles it first! There is surely a lesson here. Too readily we get involved in quarrels about all sorts of legitimate matters while we neglect the most important thing of all: our calling to live in love and unity with one another. Jesus taught that unity in love is to be the one fundamental feature of the lifestyle of believers (John 13:34, 35). Paul begins at precisely the same point. All the other matters are of no consequence alongside the need for love (see also chapter 13).

What divided the Corinthians?
Christians have discussed for centuries what lay at the heart of the divisions in Corinth but we simply do not know! Yet, perhaps, this is significant. It seems clear that Paul, Peter and Apollos, though having very different gifts and personalities, were themselves united. There is

no mention of any theological matter that divided them. Almost certainly, then, the differences were the result of personality cults, preferences for one preacher over another, especially if one of these men had been the means of the believer's conversion or baptism (14). Possibly, those who were influenced by the 'wisdom' teaching of the ancient world had come to see Apollos, a capable speaker from the most respected university town in the Mediterranean (Acts 18:24–28), as their champion. There is, however, nothing in the New Testament to suggest that he favoured such teaching.

Paul was a great pastor. Passionately he reminds his readers of the one great truth that they had so easily forgotten (10, 13). As believers in the Lord Jesus they were now brothers for whom Christ, not Paul or any other, had died. But, more than this, they were members of Christ's living body, not severed parts of a corpse! They had one Lord, having, by baptism, signified that they had become his possession.

Neglect of these great truths and a failure to work them out practically lies at the heart of so many of the divisions found both within and between churches. Our own preferences and unsanctified personalities cause splits and divisions among the people of God. The result is that we become as unsightly as a torn garment, a fact that the unbeliever is sometimes quicker to spot than we are!

What can we do?

For us, as for the Corinthians, certain steps are demanded. We are called to live in peace with one another (the meaning of *agree with one another*: verse 10). This is to be achieved by ending such dishonouring divisions.

Party spirit is to be brought to an end, something which is possible when believers have their hearts and wills united in a desire for peace. When love of peace goes together with considerable effort to achieve it marvels can be achieved! This is the apostle's point when he calls for them to be *united in mind and thought*, not that we shall ever agree on every single thing. Rather he aims at a unity which is far more deep-seated and found in the heart of every believer. The same emphasis on effort and healing is found in his call to be *perfectly united*, a phrase which was sometimes used to mean knitting together fractured bones.

Sadly, however, we spend more effort and time in falling out with one another than ever we do at building the unity which the Lord Jesus wants (John 17:20ff.). In this way we show how far we are from having the mind of Christ formed in us.

'So', says Paul, 'what does it matter who baptized whom and

whether the evangelist or teacher is eloquent or not?' (14–17). Paul would not have discouraged speaking gifts. But he knew that those very gifts can sometimes obscure the message. 'Better my halting presentation of the truth than a skilled and learned talk which entertains the mind but fails to win the heart.'

Eloquence or transformed life?

Two incidents come to the mind of the authors of this book. There was the occasion when one of us was told, shortly after assuming leadership in the church, that no-one would ever replace the leader who had died 45 years earlier! The lady who said this had every reason to remember this person with affection. However, the effect of such a conviction had been to lead to spiritual stagnation and party spirit.

The other example concerns a young woman who had often listened to an eloquent preacher who considerably moved her. Later, now in another fellowship, she confessed that she seldom had such experiences but she realized her life had changed! Various evangelical traditions today speak of unction or anointed preaching. Sometimes it appears that these words clothe precisely the fault Paul identifies here. The eloquence of the speaker must not be confused with the eloquence of the Spirit which is seen in transformed lives, not 'inspired utterance'.

Questions
1. Christians are called to be brothers and sisters. Is this true of the way I relate to other believers (especially those who are 'different' from me)? What should I do about it?
2. What are the arguments for and against going to special meetings just to hear your favourite preacher? Would Paul approve?
3. What are the priority concerns in our churches? In the light of this passage, are they the things that are at the top of God's 'agenda'?
4. Would Paul have approved of our divided denominations? What would he have advised (or commanded)?
5. What should be the difference between Christian fellowship and friendships between non-Christians?

1 Corinthians 1:18–25
The foolishness of the cross

The Corinthians were in danger of allowing the attitudes and opinions of the non-Christian world to alter the gospel message they taught. Paul warns them against an ever-present danger.

Paul's reference to words of human wisdom (17) was quite deliberate. It appears that there were people in Corinth who were rejecting Paul and his message because of his lack of oratory. Greek culture thought very highly of the able speaker. More than that, however, the Corinthians were in danger of being swamped by that culture and rejecting the very gospel itself.

A suffering God

At the heart of Greek beliefs about God was the conviction that he was without any feelings and totally distanced himself from human affairs. To preach a God who became a man and suffered, even to death, on a cross was unthinkable and quite horrifying. To such people, without the illumination of the Spirit, the gospel was 'foolishness'. The gospel, however, demonstrated the power of God since those who believed it discovered what Greek philosophers had long sought in vain (see Acts 17:32).

This came as no surprise to the apostle (19). The Old Testament Scriptures had long ago taught this very fact! Paul quotes Isaiah 29:14, one of a series of scriptures which warned that it was folly to try to match wits with God. Then, Paul asks, 'in the light of what God has done on the cross, where is your much vaunted wisdom?' (20). Just as God's vindication of Isaiah overthrew all the strategies of the wise counsellors of his day, so the gospel confounds Paul's modern counterparts (Isaiah 33:18), *the philosopher* (disputer) *of the age.* Such 'wisdom' is part of a sinful world order which is in decay.

The Greek world, for all its learning, had no real knowledge of God, not least because it saw no need of salvation from sin (21). However, those who were made conscious of their need and had welcomed the gospel had found what, for all its learning, the Greek world still groped after (22).

A crucified Messiah

Paul knew that this is always the story of men and women who start with themselves and try to discover God along their own paths. If the Greeks were in darkness so were the Jews. For them, however, there were two quite different problems. They had very clear ideas of what to expect from their Messiah: he would be a powerful political leader who would rescue them from the Roman emperor. He would major in the spectacular as, they believed, all God's servants had always done!

Secondly, the idea of a suffering Messiah who would die on a cross was inconceivable to them. 'After all,' they reasoned, 'Moses' law teaches that the person who is hanged is under the curse of God' (23: see Deuteronomy 21:23). The Christian message thus offered a totally impossible view of God to Jews and Gentiles alike.

People, however, who put their faith in the crucified Messiah find new life and also the power to lead it (24). Even God's 'poorest shot' condemns the most elevated thoughts of unbelieving men to the rubbish bin (25)!

The particular forms of unbelief change from age to age but Paul's verdict is no less relevant to the follies of today than it was to those of the first century. Despite this, the church down the ages has consistently fallen into the Corinthian error. Time and again it has tried to avoid the scandal of the cross and has ended up proclaiming a message devoid of power, unable to meet the deepest needs of men and women, and it has emptied the churches. The world in general may continue to laugh at the Christian message but to those whom God is saving its proclamation remains one of life from the dead.

Questions
1. By trying to be inoffensive to non-Christians, am I in danger of failing to hold fast to the gospel? How can I keep the balance?
2. How hard should we try to make the gospel acceptable to people today?

3. Why are the world's fashions of thought (e.g., superstitions, demands for scientific proof) held so passionately? What will help people to change their wrong opinions?

Greek religion and philosophy

Paul was correct to say of the Athenians, *I see that in every way you are very religious* (Acts 17:22). But this was not only true of Athenians; it characterized the entire known world at the time. Religions included everything from the state-controlled worship of the emperor to the ecstatic mystery religions.

The Greek-speaking world was also dominated by a deep interest in philosophical thinking and debate, fuelled (as it often was) through skilled debate among professional debaters. The greatest of the speakers were feted as pop-stars or TV personalities are today.

Much of the New Testament is set in this mixture of religious and philosophical views. This is certainly true of 1 Corinthians where certain of the views held by the false teachers seem to be derived from a religious philosophy which later developed into a movement known as Gnosticism. Paul's rejection, for example, of eloquence and superior wisdom (see especially 1:18 – 2:16) seems to reflect his refusal to accommodate Christianity to the pagan religious and philosophical ethos of his day.

Paul could use pagan religion as a starting point in evangelism, as in Acts 17:22–31. This reminds us of the way in which he gives his own interpretation to the Corinthians' favourite ideas about wisdom, knowledge and the spiritual life, all drawn from pagan thought. But Paul's basic attitude is clear from Ephesians 4:17–18: 'The Gentiles live futile lives and think futile thoughts; all their thought processes are darkened by ignorance because they are separated from God'.

1 Corinthians 1:26–31

The foolishness of God's people

God's message may not appear very sophisticated and neither may his disciples! But this is so typical of God; he does not deal with the proud!

The 'foolish' gospel message is able to do what clever human philosophies utterly fail to achieve; it saves people (26)! It was this very fact, confirmed by their own experience, that the Corinthians were in danger of forgetting ('Think,' says the apostle!). God might have chosen to put the gospel in a form which would have appealed mainly to educated and intelligent people. As the sovereign God he could have ensured that large numbers of wealthy and important people were converted. That would certainly have been the case if a human being had been in charge of the plan of salvation! However, if this had happened most of the Corinthians would still have been unbelievers. But God had chosen most of them when they were slaves or freedmen: foolish, weak and 'nothings' (27, 28).

This description of the Corinthians is a vivid reminder of the conditions under which many men and women lived in the time of Paul. There were over sixty million slaves in the Roman empire. Such people, though often well treated and gifted, had the same status as an animal or a tool. An old slave could be flung out by his or her master like a worn-out spade or fork. The master could amuse himself by torturing or even killing his slaves. Even the slave's children belonged to the master and could be disposed of as he saw fit. These people really were 'nothings' but, from what we know of the early church, the first congregations were largely drawn from among such people. Thus, most of the names known to us were common slave-names or were used among the lower classes.

In this way God demonstrated that he was determined to undermine all human pride and boasting (29). So he not only called 'non-people' but, through Jesus' death on the cross, created a people who manifested a 'new life and love, new purity and peace, new hope and happiness' within one of the most debauched and degraded cities in the ancient world. Thus, Jesus was demonstrated as true wisdom, and boasting in anything else than him and his death was shown to be an empty shell, a tinsel-covered but empty box (31: Paul quotes Jeremiah 9:23–24).

The tragedy was, however, that the Corinthians were in danger of forgetting all of this and becoming entranced with the clever rhetoric, empty words and powerless human philosophies of unbelievers who had despised and rejected them and their God long ago!

Men and women today find all sorts of reasons to reject God. But, at heart, the problem is always pride. Sometimes they come up with the most sophisticated arguments for unbelief and, as Christians, we can become confused or think that, like the Corinthians, we need eloquent responses or require fresh ways to present the truth. We should not despise Christians with such abilities and we should always try to be relevant without 'watering down' the gospel message. However, it is more important simply to point to the fact that at the cross we have found what the world has never discovered for all its fine words and learned discussions. We have found forgiveness and power to live a new life.

Questions

1. How ought I to be challenged by the fact that God often uses people who seem to lack natural gifts and abilities?
2. Why do you think Paul chose those four lovely words to describe Jesus in verse 30? What do they mean? How do we experience these things in Jesus?
3. Do you think that poor people are more likely to become Christians than rich people? Does God have a special love for the poor? If so, what can we do about it?

1 Corinthians 2:1–5
The foolishness of the preacher

It is not only the message and the followers of the gospel which some-times appear foolish but the messengers too. But God's power is seen in lives changed by the gospel.

Paul affirms that his own ministry among the Corinthians was consistent with the principles which he has been teaching in 1:18–31. He does so with much tenderness, addressing his readers in terms of great affection as 'brothers'(1). He may find it necessary to be stern with the Corinthian church but his motive is his deep love for them and his desire to keep them in the true faith. He sets us all a good example. So, he reminds his readers of what most of them must have known firsthand: in his ministry among them he had rejected everything that hinted at self-reliance. He did not preach to draw attention to himself either in the content ('superior wisdom') or the form ('eloquence') of what he said. His sole purpose was to pass on God's message, his testimony, to his hearers.

This is an important enough point for Paul to explain himself more fully (2). Long before he had arrived in Corinth he had decided on his evangelistic strategy and to do without the rhetorical or philosophical flourishes of Greek 'wisdom'. That decision involved him in proclaiming the most scandalous of all truths to the Greek thinker, the humiliating crucifixion of Christ. He was prepared to insist on this scandal because it lay at the very heart of the gospel, the testimony of God. The death of Christ as an atonement for sinners determined the whole content of his preaching.

Paul's poor image
But it was not just the content and style of his ministry which rejected Greek wisdom. As a preacher himself he had no obvious ability (3). The

Corinthians knew this only too well since some were criticizing him for it (2 Corinthians 10:10). However, Paul turns these criticisms on their heads. During his stay in Corinth he had apparently suffered from ill-health. This doubtless gave him a somewhat unimpressive appearance. But this was not all for, as he explains with great honesty, he was full of fear. Perhaps a Christian who has been in similar circumstances can feel with Paul. Thus John Calvin writes, 'he was surrounded by many dangers, he was in perpetual fear and constant anxiety'. It is also possible that Paul was overwhelmed by the task of evangelizing the city (Acts 18:9–11), shy in the face of strange surroundings (Acts 17:15; 18:5) or, perhaps, he was anxiously awaiting news (2 Corinthians 2:13). Whatever it was he felt vulnerable and even the message itself seems to have caused him anxiety, making him feel inadequate to preach it.

The message was so 'foolish' and the preacher so poor that the birth of the Corinthian church must have been a marvellous work of God by his Spirit alone (4, 5). There are certain things that cannot be faked, supremely the evidence of changed lives especially in a polluted and depraved city like Corinth. Paul implies that wisdom can produce intellectual conviction of truth but it is powerless to create a living, transforming faith in God. In this way the gospel is verified.

The power of the Spirit

When Paul writes of the *demonstration of the Spirit's power* his first thought is of the faith that was created in men and women when they heard the word of God (5). It is unlikely that he is thinking of 'signs and wonders' because he is emphasizing weakness here. However, he probably does have in mind both the creation of faith and the gifts of the Spirit which had been received when the Corinthians were converted. Later Paul will have occasion to touch upon the issue of Christian ministry again (4:11–13; 2 Corinthians 2:14 – 6:13).

Paul is not merely reflecting upon an incident in the past. What he has to say is seen as a model for ministry in every age of the Christian church. The paragraph is the touchstone of all true preaching.

We, too, need to grasp that true preaching is not found in the use of clever techniques or styles or in a manner which panders to the desires of the hearers. True preaching is a simple witness to what God has done in Jesus by the cross. It is seen to be 'of the Spirit' not by the intellectual or emotional impact it has upon its hearers but in the evidence of changed lives. Indeed, sometimes the sheer brilliance of an address can obscure the message. Not infrequently the brilliance of an illustration is remembered long afterwards but the point made is soon forgotten.

Questions

1. 'I believe the gospel.' How exactly does that faith give me encouragement today?
2. How do we assess a good sermon in our churches?
3. What will convince the non-Christian world of the truth of the gospel? Will signs and wonders?

1 Corinthians 2:6–10a
The riches all believers share

The Corinthians were being offered a 'special' gospel by some false teachers who claimed there was more to the Christian message than Paul taught. Paul reminds his readers of all the privileges that 'his' gospel had brought them.

Reading this letter is rather like listening to someone speaking on the telephone. The words are heard, but their precise meaning is not easy to understand because we can't hear the other end of the conversation. This is especially true in this section. We know that Paul was responding to a letter which he had received (see discussion on 1:1–3, pp. 14–15) and we also know the ideas which were popular in Corinth at the time. Both these factors influenced Paul. But it is still hard to be certain exactly what he is teaching.

The church has always been plagued by those who have claimed that the 'mere gospel' is only a stepping stone to 'deeper teaching' and a 'higher life'. Such claims were apparently being made in Corinth since as we read Paul's words it seems that we can hear echoes of some of the favourite phrases of the false teachers. They claimed to teach a message for the 'mature' (6); a teaching which revealed *the deep things of God* (10) to the *spiritual man* (15).

In addition, in the Corinthian church there were those who believed that wisdom was to be found in philosophy and eloquence (see 1:18–25). We catch some of their phrases in the language Paul uses here. They spoke about 'mysterious wisdom' which had been 'hidden' (7) from the majority of believers who were 'fleshly men' (14) and who were enslaved in ignorance to imaginary spiritual *rulers of this age* (8). They even seem to have quoted Scripture (verse 9 quotes from Isaiah 64:41, a passage widely misused among the mystery religions of the time).

The cross is vital

It all sounded very attractive and plausible (as 'higher life' teaching invariably does), but Paul forthrightly rejects these beliefs (6) using their own language but altogether changing its meaning. He does not despise learning or suggest that the Christian message was foolish nonsense. The Christian message is 'wisdom' but of a totally different sort from the Corinthians' 'wisdom'. Paul uses one of their own catchwords, 'mature', which they used to speak of a special wisdom that was the prerogative of the few. But he transforms its meaning to apply to all those who are truly living as Christians.

Paul's argument now runs like this in verses 7–8. 'It is true', he says, 'that the gospel I preach can be described in words that you yourselves use, a "mystery", something which was "hidden" for many centuries. However, it is a mystery which has been revealed in the incarnation and crucifixion of Jesus and brings benefits to all God's people. There were of course those who did not realize this. You speak of people as blinded by "the rulers of this age" but you are speaking of imaginary spiritual beings. I, however, do not speak about some mythical invention but of those political and intellectual leaders who invented the ideas you are chasing. *They* put to death the very one who radiated in his person the glory of God in a bodily form. What folly, then, to allow your ideas about what are spiritual men to be influenced by such blind guides!'

Paul continues his argument by appealing to a scripture which appears to have been a favourite passage of his opponents (9). It was an amalgamation of Old Testament texts based on Isaiah 64:4 and spoke of the inconceivable greatness of those things which God has in store for his people. Doubtless the Corinthian false teachers would have used these words to bolster their own views about hidden mysteries revealed only to the few.

However, Paul notes that in the gospel these things are now revealed through the agency of the Holy Spirit (10a). This leads him to discuss more fully the work of the Holy Spirit and to demonstrate conclusively the bankruptcy of thinking which is blind to spiritual realities and the genuine wisdom of the gospel (10b–16). Note that in verse 6 Paul pointedly changed from speaking of 'I' to using the word 'us'. This is very significant. He had been accused of being a teacher of mere 'milk' (3:1), of being among the 'fleshly men'. His opponents put him in a group from which they excluded themselves. Paul, however, at precisely this point, uses an inclusive word: *us*. In this very pointed way he rejects any notion of different classes of Christians. In the gospel of Christ crucified *all* the riches of God have been revealed to *all* true believers.

Many Christians live rootless lives and are constantly seeking some sort of key which will unlock for them a fuller and deeper experience of God. We need to learn the lesson which Paul teaches here: spiritual growth sprouts from the foot of the cross, not from some territory on the other side. We can never get beyond the cross. Moreover, it is significant that Paul cites a scripture which concludes with the words 'to those who love him' (9). It is not knowledge but love which is the mark of true maturity and spirituality (see chapter 13), and it is love which arouses God to reveal more of himself in the cross by his Spirit.

Questions
1. Do I fully realize the privileges that are mine as a result of my believing the gospel? What are they?
2. How do 'we all' receive revelation from/through the Holy Spirit? Shall we really understand God's wisdom when we are 'mature'?
3. What false ideas that are found in the non-Christian world are influencing Christian thinking today?

1 Corinthians 2:10b–16
Wisdom from the Spirit

Christians often have a poor understanding of the work of the Holy Spirit. Paul corrects the errors of the Corinthians.

 Paul has just established that the gospel of Christ crucified reveals the wisdom of God to all believers. In this paragraph he explains how those who are regarded as great thinkers reject the gospel, the wisdom of God, as sheer foolishness. He does so to reassure those who might feel inferior in the face of the world's opinions and be in danger, as many were, of capitulation. His lesson has a lasting relevance to many today who are hemmed in by destructive talk about the Christian gospel, even talk within the professing church. In addition, however, by doing this Paul also shows that, for all their talk about 'spiritual' things, his opponents had a weak view of the person and work of the Holy Spirit. Behind this fact lay a failure to understand properly the serious plight of mankind. Opposition to the gospel so often arises at this point. Men and women, ignorant of their true need, are quick to criticize a message which does not address them where they like to think they are!

We need the Spirit's help to understand the truth
Paul begins with a very simple illustration (10b–11). In his day 'spirit' was a word used of the whole of a person's inner life, including the mind. No-one, he says, knows fully what is going on in another person's head other than the person himself or herself! So it is with God! His Spirit alone knows all that there is to be known about him. But believers receive as a free and unearned gift the Spirit of God when they become Christians. Consequently, they have the ability to perceive the wisdom of God (12).

So Paul and his companions, and Christians today, teach as God's Spirit directs, not with philosophical ideas or the rhetorical flourishes that appeal to unbelieving men and women (13). Such an approach, he realizes, does not appeal to those who do not see things spiritually (13, 14). It is important to understand Paul at this point. He does not mean people who are unintelligent or wicked but simply men and women who lack the illumination which the Spirit alone gives. To this day, the Christian message is still often regarded as stupid. The reason for this remains the same: unless God gives his Spirit it is impossible to appreciate the message of the gospel.

The problem is that, without the Spirit, people are like those who try to find their way through a vast city with only a fragment of a street plan (15–16). It is not that people's ideas are necessarily evil so much as inadequate and by nature incapable of perceiving the truth. However, illuminated by the Spirit, the Christian can understand the world, its needs and God's answer. The Christian can recognize the gospel message for the wisdom it truly is.

So the person without the Spirit is not in a position to criticize the beliefs of a Christian. On the contrary, the believer has the key to judging the beliefs of the world. In a nutshell, God doesn't need us to advise him as to what is wise or not and believers need not worry about what outsiders say about the gospel, for they, the believers, are the ones in whom Christ Jesus lives by the Spirit.

The basic point that Paul is making throughout this section is that people are revealed for what they truly are by their reaction to the crucifixion.

A summary

It is worth summarizing what Paul is saying here. It is the Spirit who first enables a person to receive, understand and appreciate the wisdom of God and it is the same Spirit who enables the believer to come to understand and pass on the gospel message. Without his ministry no communication is possible between God and his people and no growth to maturity is possible.

We do well to ensure that we have fully understood Paul, since several errors have been based upon a failure properly to grasp what he is teaching. He teaches that the gift of the Spirit does not make a distinction between Christians but between believers and unbelievers; he rejects any idea of class or caste distinctions among believers and emphasizes that being 'spiritual' leads to a proper understanding of the scandal of the cross.

Notice that there is no suggestion here that Christians can go through life with the conceited notion that since they are led by the Spirit they must always be right. Nor does this passage teach that the believer need not study or use his or her mind but will be infallibly led by the Spirit in everything. No, Paul simply emphasizes that without the Spirit the excellence and wisdom of the gospel can be neither perceived nor received by unbelievers.

Questions

1. In the light of this passage, what should I understand of the work of the Holy Spirit?
2. How do we have the 'mind of Christ' (verse 16)? Do we learn it from his teaching recorded in the gospels or does the Holy Spirit give it directly to us?
3. What are the real needs of non-Christians today as outlined in this passage?

THE CHURCH AND ITS MINISTRY

1 Corinthians 3:1–23

1 Corinthians 3:1–4
Spirituality into division won't go!

Paul is faced with a church that thinks it is spiritual when in fact it is divided. He shows that the two things cannot exist side by side.

Paul has spent chapters 1 and 2 discussing two issues. He has mentioned the divisions which exist in the Corinthian church and he has also discussed the false teachers who claimed to have knowledge of a superior form of the gospel. In this passage he begins to show that these are part of the same problem.

Paul is both pastoral and blunt (these two do sometimes go together!). He calls his readers 'brothers' but goes on to insist that they are living as though they were babies, not grown ups (1)! We can probably hear the language of Paul's opponents in the words 'worldly' (a better translation is 'merely human') and 'milk'; this was what they claimed about Paul's teaching (2). By comparison they were claiming to offer 'solid food' which was 'spiritual'.

Paul's response is to agree with their verdict on his teaching; it was basic gospel truth dispensed in a form that was digestible to recent converts. However, he points out that they are still not ready for anything else (3), because they are continuing to live as though they were unredeemed human beings who were strangers to the transforming effects of the gospel. This is obvious for it is seen in their petty squabbles (4). Far from being 'mature' Christians they were showing by the way they lived that they were mere 'babies in Christ'.

As believers we are often faced with groups who offer what they claim is a 'superior' form of Christianity to that which we follow. This can be perplexing. It is, perhaps, encouraging to discover that this problem is not a new one. The true believer is, of course, concerned to go on to maturity and so such claims are often very attractive. But how can we tell whether or not such things are from God? We can learn a great deal from the way Paul handled the situation in Corinth.

The danger of 'Christianity plus'

False teaching often offers a Christianity *plus*. Paul rejects this. Such teaching is, itself, the mark of immaturity for it fails to find the gospel all-sufficient (see below). It often offers a Christianity which leaves the cross behind (compare 1:18). But Paul emphasizes that there is no truly Christian experience beyond the cross. The Christian life begins and continues alone at the foot of the cross.

Then, false teaching often neglects true holiness. Claiming to be 'spiritual', these people were living according to the standards of the unbelieving world.

Finally, such teaching is frequently accompanied by a divisive spirit. Often this is accompanied by personality cults (even if the leaders themselves would not support their 'alleged' disciples), where the leaders are exalted over Christ. Yet, we notice that these things are not necessarily the marks of heresy but rather of immaturity (1, 2). Such people were not unspiritual but they were immature. They needed careful discipling, not expulsion.

Paul's teaching here is not all negative. He teaches that a maturing faith builds upon the gospel itself. The contrast in Paul's mind between 'milk' and 'solid food' is one of degree. The letter as a whole shows that it is by an ever-deepening grasp of the gospel first received that growth occurs.

A maturing faith is seen in a 'superhuman' lifestyle. Paul expects the true believer to manifest increasingly a quality of life that the unsaved world cannot copy. It is something which only the indwelling Spirit (= spiritual) can produce. Such a maturing faith is seen not in the exalting of others or of self but in honouring Christ (compare 1:1ff.), and is demonstrated, above all, in a peaceable spirit.

Paul may have been dealing with a specific situation in Corinth but we can learn a great deal from both the situation and his response to it.

Questions
1. Paul says that bad living hinders deep learning (2, 3). Why is this? Can you think of other ways in which sin stops us from understanding our faith?
2. Are there divisions in your church? If so, how might the lessons of this passage apply to the situation?
3. Christians are expected to witness to the unbelieving world by living 'supernatural lives'. How far is this true of us?

1 Corinthians 3:5–9

Only servants

All Christian workers are expected to work together under the blessing of God. There can, therefore, be no place for 'favourites' and 'parties'.

 The Corinthian church, as we have seen, had been foolishly divided over which leader they preferred. Paul indicates that there was nothing 'wise' or 'spiritual' about this (5). In fact, it showed that the congregation had completely failed to understand what the church was and how leaders were expected to function within the fellowship. In responding to the church, Paul says several things that remain both vital and neglected today. Each leader, he says, is called by God: *the Lord has assigned to each his task.*

Each leader is called to servanthood. They are servants of God but (as this passage indicates) they are also servants of the church. Paul uses a word which could also mean 'waiter'. It is a word, too, which emphasizes active service. A Christian leader must be active in undertaking God's calling.

Each leader has been given different responsibilities and functions by God. Paul gives a relevant example (6). He had planted the church at Corinth but Apollos (supported by some as an alternative leader) had provided the ongoing evangelistic support the church needed.

Most important of all, the success of every Christian servant is entirely in the hands of God (7). Whatever Paul and Apollos may have done, it was God who was at work to produce fruit. As a result of this, it is God who ought to be given honour and praise, not the mere 'table waiters'.

Since each leader is doing the work God has appointed, they are working to achieve the same end within the church of God (8). In verse 9 'God' is mentioned three times; the emphasis throughout is upon God and not personalities.

The lesson is obvious: to prefer one 'waiter' to another is foolish in itself but to do so when the work of each is necessary to complete the task that God is undertaking is utter stupidity and very far from being 'spiritual'.

Questions
1. Do your own personal likes and dislikes in Christian leaders threaten to become so large that you effectively deny that someone is doing God's will? How can you prevent this from happening?
2. Does your church see different gifts as evidence of the grace of God or a basis for criticizing the people who haven't got the gifts that others consider important? Where can we strike the balance?
3. Sometimes there is wisdom to be learnt from non-Christians! They don't honour waiters! Do we? Discuss some examples.

1 Corinthians 3:10–15
Building with care

Leaders within the church are to lead in serving and they are to make sure they do it well lest they are judged by their failure.

With these verses Paul offers specific guidance to the leaders of the church in Corinth. He reminds them that, with the skill and attention to detail of a good architect, he had been given the privilege of planting the church at Corinth (10). It was all of God's grace and none of Paul's own doing.

However, God's servants do not all occupy the same function and that foundation was now being built upon by others. This was fine since the local church is to be always on the move; building is to be always in progress.

Nevertheless, great care was needed in the building work. In particular, proper foundations (the ones already laid by the apostle) were vital and the proper materials were necessary to ensure a lasting work of real value. This alone was the basis for the church being established and nurtured with 'wisdom'.

First of all, Paul reminds the Corinthians that there can be only one foundation (11). The gospel of the Lord Jesus Christ, the person and work of the Saviour are the only basis upon which any church fellowship can be established.

This emphasis upon Christian basics was doubtless deliberate. It is characteristic of all 'higher life' forms of teaching to direct the attention of their followers elsewhere (without necessarily meaning to!). Paul offers a test by which the presence of false emphases could be recognized within the church; it is a test that is ever relevant.

With verse 12 the direction of Paul's comments changes. His point is that not only must the foundation be the correct one but appropriate materials must be used to undertake the building work. The contrast he makes appears to be between durable and perishable materials. It is probably significant that the materials mentioned here which adorned the temple, gold, silver and precious stones, are durable. Paul suggests that a church (that is, the people) discipled effectively upon the foundation of the gospel is one that has eternal value, adorning and glorifying the name of the Lord.

However, it is only too possible, as Paul recognized, that incompetent workmen can ruin a building work (13). Some of these materials may, at first, appear to be ideal; a wooden structure can look more impressive than one of precious metals and stones. But if the wrong materials are used the lasting usefulness is nil. It is the God-given, not the merely human, that is to be pursued. Unaided human endeavour collapses like a building made of hay or stubble.

With this in mind Paul offers a solemn warning to the leaders at Corinth. He reminds them that one day God will judge the work that every leader has undertaken. He likens the judgment to a fire which consumes all but the most imperishable of materials.

Sadly, he implies that when that day comes, some church leaders will discover that all their efforts have been wasted (14). While they themselves will not suffer judgment (because their actions were not deliberate or heretical but only misguided and erroneous: verse 15) they will find that there is nothing of value that they can take into the life to come. Indeed, Paul may even suggest that so close has their folly taken them to the brink of their own personal destruction they will, as it were, feel the scorching heat of the judgment themselves!

Questions
1. Are there trivial 'truths' that I pursue rather than building upon the great truth of the gospel? How can I tell the difference?
2. What sort of church 'building' do you think Paul has in mind with each of these types of materials? Give examples.
3. What silver, gold and precious stones do you think you and your fellowship will be able to present to Jesus when he returns?

1 Corinthians 3:16–23
Christ is the head and source of all things

Paul reminds his readers of the true nature of the church.

Having addressed the congregation (1–9), Paul turned to speak to the leaders (10–15), warning them to make sure that they led the church correctly. In both these sections he was concerned to ensure that both church and leadership had a proper understanding of the nature of true Christian leadership.

In verse 16 Paul shifts his attention to another vital, but related, matter. The church, Paul reminds his readers, is the sanctuary, the 'home' of the only true God and, consequently, the Spirit of God was present in the midst of the church. In a wickedly sinful city the church at Corinth was the only place where God was to be found, a people set apart as his dwelling ('holy'). But this temple could be desecrated and destroyed through party spirit and quarrelling.

This was a serious possibility since one act of destruction would bring about another; those who destroyed the church would be destroyed in judgment themselves (17). Their punishment would fit the crime! The false teacher was in danger of passing on to his or her eternal destiny naked but secure (15). Here, however, is the suggestion that where such error becomes the basis for destruction of the church (whether advanced by teacher or pupil) then even that security is stripped away; eternal punishment alone awaits the architect of such destruction! We should note Paul's exalted view of the local church, and the severity of the warning contained in his words!

So the apostle reaches his conclusion (18). The problem which he had described is seen as rooted in the 'wisdom' teaching which was making inroads into the church. Paul is abrupt; 'wisdom' such teaching might be, but only according to the standards of a sinful and fallen world! That being the case, it was high time that the Corinthians who were teaching or following such teaching learnt to be 'fools', God's fools!

He reminds them that worldly wisdom is not compatible with the ways of God (he quotes Job 5:13 and Psalm 94:11). Compared to God's thoughts human thoughts, even at their best, are self-deceiving and futile (19, 20).

So he urges his readers to take God's perspective (21). This meant that they should not boast in mere table-waiters but recognize that every believer possesses everything (22, 23)! Yet such wealth is that of a steward, for it belongs to another, Christ. Paul emphasizes this by stressing that in Christ (but only in him!) the individual believer is victor over everything that tyrannizes mankind. Each of the things Paul mentions is something that, as human beings, we instinctively cling to or dread. As such they hold us in a vice-like grip. However, the believer is freed from their power; life is not all there is and death is conquered. The present is a gift from God and the future is secure in his hands!

Questions

1. If the church is the temple and dwelling place of God what implications ought this to have for me?
2. What is the 'wisdom of the world'? Explain it to each other or write out your answer.
3. In view of verse 20, should we automatically reject all the views of all 'pundits' or acclaimed leaders? How can we judge what to accept and put into practice?
4. What are the things which hold non-Christians today in a vice-like grip? How does the gospel meet such a situation?

CHRISTIAN APOSTLES
1 Corinthians 4:1–21

1 Corinthians 4:1–5
Answerable to God

Ultimately the faithful Christian worker is answerable only to God.

The Corinthian church had been vainly boasting about their preferred leaders, the folly of which Paul had eloquently exposed (chapter 3). So how should leaders be viewed?

Paul had earlier used the word 'servants' of himself and Apollos (3:5). The same basic point is made here but a different Greek word (also meaning 'servant') is used. It is likely that the choice of the word is deliberate since it was a word which emphasized the responsibility of administering the affairs of another, in this case things delegated by Christ. This understanding of the word seems to be supported by the next description, *entrusted with the secret things of God*, since the word 'entrusted' carries the thought of managing the household as the trusted steward.

Incidentally, Paul places Christ and God alongside one another. This is typical of the way the New Testament often mentions the two in the same breath. The early church had a very high view of Jesus.

But Paul's main point here is that leaders are not the possession of the local church or at its beck and call (2). Every servant or steward is required, above all, to be faithful to his responsibility and charge. In this case, the Christian leader is to be faithful in the presentation of the gospel. The Old Testament had pointed forward to it, but it was now revealed in Christ. Paul and other leaders were responsible to God to minister the gospel faithfully (3).

The criticisms that Paul had been facing in Corinth amounted to nothing short of a judicial enquiry. Though this hurt him (Paul did care 'a little'!), it was ultimately of no consequence since these were matters for God alone to judge.

Indeed, he did not even feel able to judge his own ministry (4, 5). Although his conscience did not trouble him, he recognized that there are some things, motives and attitudes, that can be hidden even from oneself. So let God alone judge when he is ready.

Paul, of course, was not suggesting that judgment is always wrong (compare 5:12; 6:5). However, when it comes to assessments of success or failure and of an individual's integrity (which seems to be what Paul is talking about) then there is only one who has the ability and right to make them. God alone fully knows the facts and has full insight into motives.

Oddly, though the Corinthians claimed to be able to judge all things (2:15), they were foolishly claiming an ability in an area outside their competence while being blind to what lay right before them (as the sequel of chapters 5 and 6 shows)!

Questions
1. How should I prepare for the moment when my inmost thoughts and motives are exposed (verse 5)?
2. Where in the life of your congregation ought judgments be made?
3. Some at Corinth disagreed with Paul's leadership. Paul asks them to recognize him as 'a servant of Christ'. Does this imply that (for instance) Protestant Christians ought to be ready to recognize the authority of the Pope? Is Paul asking us to suspend our critical judgment?

1 Corinthians 4:6–13
Authentic Christian ministry

With great irony, Paul contrasts the realities of true Christian ministry with the triumphalistic version offered by the false teachers in Corinth.

 Paul had mentioned others. The church was intended to learn ('benefit') from what he had said (6). In fact it was time for the truth to be told. The church at Corinth must learn from Paul to be humble. They were becoming so proud that they were in danger of leaving Paul behind and also the gospel itself!

The meaning of the end of verse 6 is not clear but it appears that the Corinthians were in danger of ignoring the teachings and principles of the Old Testament Scriptures. Perhaps their 'prophets' were esteeming their own words over the Old Testament and proudly exalting themselves or those with ministries more suited to their 'higher-life' tastes (7). Such claims were out of place among those who professed to be disciples of Jesus. Their claims to superiority were presumptuous; mere self-congratulation. Moreover, the very things they boasted about (doubtless their spiritual gifts and abilities) were not earned but freely given to them. So there could be no basis for such ungrateful pride.

The consequences of such an attitude spawned a belief that they had already 'arrived' spiritually and were enjoying their own private experience ('without us') of God's kingdom (8). It was as if they believed that Christ's final reign had begun already! They were convinced that they were a successful, lively, mature church, satisfied with their spirituality, leadership and quality of life together. They had settled down to the belief that they were all they could be. This had arrested their growth and made them critical of others.

Such a desire for perfection was fine. The problem was that they thought that they had arrived 'already'. Paul wishes it were so, for then the struggles in the life of faith would be a thing of the past!

The way of the cross

By way of contrast Paul describes to the Corinthians what is, essentially, the way of the cross (9), and so offers a totally different view of the spiritual life from that which was popular at Corinth.

For Christ's sake (10) and in accordance with God's will, the apostolic experience was very different. Paul recognized that the very things which the Corinthians despised in him were true. Viewed from a worldly perspective (or super-spiritual one, for it amounts to the same thing!), Paul was a failure. Drawing upon the familiar image of a victory procession which ended with the wretched captives, who were doomed to die, the apostle describes himself and his fellow apostles as just such people! They were open to the derision of humanity and the amazement of the angelic powers (with whom, apparently, the Corinthians felt they shared some common ground, speaking their languages: see 13:1).

True Christians were certainly fools from some points of view, but fools for Christ in whose service they suffered. They experienced not the Corinthian 'theology of glory' but a life almost indistinguishable from that of the Saviour. Referring to the apostles' teaching, their character and their worldly standing, Paul admits that they did not amount to much; the teaching was human folly, their character was of the sort that the Greek mind despised as weak and, consequently, they were regarded as dishonourable. Paul pleads guilty to the charges that the wise, strong and honoured Corinthians had brought against him!

With deep irony (11), Paul mentions to those who had 'already' arrived (8) that he suffered great difficulties and wants. The happy ending was still awaited as far as he was concerned and faithfulness to his commission brought constant hardship still. How far the apostles were from the false teachers who thought they were on the throne!

Paul admits not only to a scandalous experience but also to a scandalous way of life (12, 13). Greeks would have been shocked by a teacher who worked (and manually at that!) for his living. Moreover, he submitted to cursing, persecution and slander. Humility and meekness were considered marks of weakness in Greek culture.

Some interesting allusions may well lie behind the latter part of verse 13. The word 'scum' was sometimes used of the member of society who was made the scapegoat for a community's guilt. The word 'offscouring'

was also used of those valueless members of society who were sometimes offered as human sacrifices to propitiate the gods; derelicts who
were the meanest, most worthless and most easily spared members of
society. So Paul concludes his description of authentic Christian ministry!

Questions
1. What sort of leaders do you admire?
2. Should all Christian leaders support themselves financially? Why?
   Or why not?
3. Should the success of a church or an individual Christian be measured
   in terms of financial prosperity? How should it be measured?

1 Corinthians 4:14–21
Remember whose children you are!

Like a father with his children, Paul argues for the Corinthians to grow up and abandon their childish preoccupation with 'talking big', in favour of the life that the Spirit truly produces.

 After all that has been said, Paul must now regain his proper (and God-given) respect among the members of the Corinthian church. But he cannot write like one of the authoritarian and status-conscious leaders whom he has criticized, so he makes an appeal on the basis of his love for them (14). This places him in a very vulnerable position, yet there is no alternative for someone who is not willing to play the game by the false teachers' rules. Even in his conduct as a leader his approach is dictated by his theology of the cross.

Paul appeals to his founding of the church in Corinth and his being the one through whom many of the congregation had come to faith (15). This gave him a unique position within the church as its 'father'.

So the apostle appeals to the Corinthians' loyalty as his offspring. He has, at least, a right to be listened to. In particular, he encourages them to embrace the theology of the cross that characterizes his own life (just as a child is expected to follow the example of its parent). Thus, this is not a call to rally to his 'party' but to rally to him because he is modelling Christ to them.

A gentle spirit or a big stick?
Paul hoped to visit Corinth soon (see 19), but meanwhile Timothy was planning to call at the city (17). He emphasizes that Timothy, himself a true and loved spiritual son, is fully equipped to be his representative and, as such, deserves a hearing.

59

But Paul wants to say more; the message of the gospel is a matter not merely of words but of conduct, a *way of life in Christ Jesus*. It was wrong for them to exalt themselves over other congregations of God's people (compare, also, 14:36–38). This was further evidence of spiritual pride.

Paul was aware that some of the false teachers thought that he was too spineless to face them and saw his sending Timothy as evidence of this weakness (18).

When God opened the way for him, however, Paul intended to come (19, 20). Then he would uncover the reality behind the false teachers' claims. He believed that their talk would prove to be only words, unable to bring spiritual life or sustain spiritual growth. They might speak wisdom but it would prove powerless to effect real change in people, whereas his message had all the hallmarks of the power of God released (despite its lack of conformity to what they expected and looked for). In this way Paul challenges the false teachers, not on their grounds but his own. Like children they were 'talking big' but had no power to put their words into action. So the Corinthians were to stop boasting and grow up!

If they failed in this, then when 'father' Paul arrived he would find it necessary to express his love through the rebuke of the rod rather than 'gentle' fellowship (21).

Questions
1. Am I more interested in the ideas of Christianity than in living it out? How can I keep a balance?
2. Paul insists that the Corinthians should imitate him and follow his leadership. Should all Christian ministers do the same? Why or why not?
3. What does 'power' mean to the the world? What does it mean to the church? What relevance does this have to you?

FAILED
CHRISTIANITY
1 Corinthians 5:1 – 6:20

1 Corinthians 5:1–5
Blind to the obvious!

The Corinthians were so conceited about their spiritual status that they could not see their serious sin. Paul has to burst the bubble!

Throughout his letter Paul has been seeking to expose the arrogance of the Corinthian believers who claimed to be on a different spiritual plane from everybody else. In the previous chapter he concludes that their failures at the level of what they do reveal that their teaching is mere words. These mere words have none of the power that accompanies faithful trust in the gospel of Jesus, the crucified one.

The Roman empire was renowned for its permissiveness and within that empire Corinth was a byword for sinful excess. Nevertheless, within the congregation at Corinth was a man who was indulging in a relationship that even the depraved world around condemned (although occasional parallels are documented in ancient books but with the deepest disapproval). This was an uncontested fact ('actually') which possibly had wide circulation outside the church (1).

The precise sin is not easy for us to determine. However, the reference to 'father's wife' rather than 'mother' suggests 'step-mother'. In addition, since the word 'adultery' is not used, it seems likely that the charge is one of incest. The phrase, *has his father's wife,* suggests a relationship which was more than a casual and illicit one. Consequently, it would appear that the man being discussed had entered into a marriage or common-law relationship with his father's wife, perhaps with his father's consent, a *ménage à trois.* 'After all,' they argued, 'if the spiritual life is all that matters, who cares what we do with our bodies?' This, then, was the situation Paul had to address.

The church's response to scandal

Yet his greater concern was with the way the church had handled the situation. There are two possible interpretations of verse 2. The Corinthians were proud either *despite* or *because of* the sinful offence. Thus, they were either so conceited that the sin was something about which they were indifferent, or proud of this man's sin because they saw it as a demonstration of their freedom in Christ. Either way their arrogant assumption that they were highly spiritual had blinded them to the presence and reality of sin. They should have been in mourning as over a death but were, in fact, rejoicing in their highly spiritual status.

There is a very contemporary ring to all of this! When we begin to think we deserve God's grace, and where grace is perceived as merited and blessing is seen as evidence of God's favour, it is easy to ignore the presence and seriousness of sin. Too many believers who have thought themselves to be 'somebody' have ended in sinful failure and are often incapable of seeing that they were in the wrong. Paul's response is that the fellowship must excommunicate the sinful brother.

The details of verses 3 and 4 are hard to understand because Paul's words can be interpreted in different ways. However, there are several points that are clear.

First of all, Paul emphasizes that discipline is to be undertaken by the congregation in the name and with the authority of Jesus. While he indicates his own view (and very strongly at that!) and expects his opinion to be followed as his 'spirit' is present while his words are read, yet it is the church gathered that is to take the necessary steps.

Secondly, this discipline is to be undertaken for the sake of the sinner, to awaken the man to his condition. The church leaders were not to be vindictive but to act out of deep grief and loving concern.

The meaning of verse 5 is also difficult. It is possible that to 'hand over to Satan' suggests physical suffering and even death. However, Paul probably means that the church's ban will effectively place the man back in the world, the domain where Satan rules. It is hoped that such an action will lead to a deep and genuine repentance which will effect a real and radical break with the sinful nature which has ensnared the man in sin.

Interestingly, this verse emphasizes the limited power of Satan. The man is handed over to Satan not so that he can do whatever he wants with the sinner, but so that he can be used as a tool in the interests of Jesus to bring about the man's salvation.

Questions

1. Do I suffer from the spiritual pride that Paul describes here? In what way(s)?

2. Under what circumstances should a church treat a member as Paul suggests here (see Matthew 18:15–17)?

3. Read 1 Corinthians 1:4–9 again. How does the episode we have just studied square with Paul's earlier description of the church?

4. In what ways does the church scandalize the non-Christian world of today?

1 Corinthians 5:6–8
Be what you are!

Paul reminds the Corinthians that the holy life is one to which they were called and one for which they are empowered.

Despite the seriousness of the sin described in verses 1–5, Paul's greatest concern remains the church. Having demonstrated the truth of his earlier judgment of the Corinthians he bluntly concludes, *Your boasting is not good!* (6).

However, there is more to be said. The church must engage in discipline for the sake of the sinner but it must also do so for its own sake. Whether Paul has the incestuous relationship still in view or whether what he condemns is the Corinthians' pride matters little, for his point is of general relevance. Quoting what appears to have been a popular proverb based upon a daily experience, Paul makes the point that sin is cancerous. Where it is not rooted out completely it spreads and infects everything.

So Paul calls for specifically Christian action (7). As Christians we are required to act in a way which conforms with God's will for us. Yet, of ourselves, the demand is something well beyond our achieving. However, it is precisely because we are in a living relationship with Christ that we are able (bit by painful bit) to become what, as to status, we already are.

It is said that spring cleaning originated with the Jewish practice of getting rid of 'leaven' once a year. Leaven was a small portion of dough which was added to new dough and, through fermentation, gave lightness to sour-dough bread. The danger of infection increased week by week and once a year a completely new batch of dough was made and the old leaven disposed of. Usually this occurred prior to the celebration of Passover. It is this that lies behind Paul's words. Sin left unchecked is like leaven and can infect the whole of the church. It needs to be thrown out.

Once more illustrating Jesus' work by the history and events of the Old Testament, Paul proceeds to offer a challenge (8). But, typically, he begins by defining 'old' and 'new' leaven in terms of attitudes and conduct. 'Wicked' conduct, the result of an underlying sinful attitude 'malice'), is to be exchanged for a life of integrity grounded in an inner purity.

Thus, the letter which began with a call to radical holiness (1:2) picks up the theme again, for it is never far from the apostle's mind. So Christians daily celebrate the fact that the Passover lamb has been slain, living as those renewed by the Spirit of God and free indeed to serve the Lord Jesus!

Questions

1. How far does what I do reflect what I really am inside? Make a list of things you enjoy and do not enjoy doing. Then ask yourself, 'Am I the person I thought I was?'
2. How does your church emphasize the power of Christ available to those who are Christians?
3. Do non-Christians see us as festive people? If not, why not?

1 Corinthians 5:9–13
Evading the truth

This was not the first time that Paul had had to rebuke the Corinthians but, in the past, they had tried not to listen!

Paul had previously written the church a letter of which we have no record apart from his comments here. In that letter, he had reminded the Corinthians that they should not have fellowship with sexually immoral people (9).

Some of those who had received the letter had, however (apparently deliberately), misunderstood his comments (10). Arguing that it was impossible not to rub shoulders with immoral people, they had considered Paul's advice to be absurd, with the result that they had allowed sinful misconduct to flourish unchecked in the church. Paul will have none of this! He explains himself, as we might say, in words of one syllable.

Corinth was a desperately wicked city, as the list of sins Paul gives here shows. Bestial and selfish attitudes and actions and rebellion against God were to be found on every street corner. This revealed itself in every form of sexual perversion, in materialism and in idolatry. It was simply impossible to escape from such an environment, since it forced its way in from every side. Paul recognizes this fact only too well!

While it may be impossible to escape being in the world, however, there was every reason to exclude the world from the church (11). Again Paul lists the sins which were prevalent in the city of Corinth (adding 'slanderer' and 'drunkard'). Altogether he emphasizes five areas which are often snares to the world and the church alike; sex, money, possessions, drink and the tongue. We need to watch the inroads of these and other sins quite as much as the Corinthians.

Paul may be hinting again that contact with such people in everyday dealings is to be discouraged, though he does not seem to be referring specifically to this issue. More probably, he teaches 'freedom of association' outside the church (despite the dangers we do well to be alert to!). However, his main point is that in the case of someone within the fellowship ('brother') living in such a sinful way, disciplinary action was imperative. In fact any action which might be seen to condone such sinful practices must be avoided at all costs.

The Corinthians had, doubtless, excused their own inactivity on the basis that they had no authority to act as judges against the practices found in their city (though they had the responsibility of taking the word of God to them). Paul does not deny that they were powerless to change the world around them and that the matter must needs be left in God's hands. However, within the church they could and ought to act and do so speedily (12, 13)!

Bluntly, Paul sets aside all evasions. The Corinthians were to face up to their God-given responsibilities and act rather than hide behind careful but spurious arguments. His point is of enduring relevance!

Interestingly, Paul seems to quote Deuteronomy 22:21 in the final verse but changes the pronouns to the plural, emphasizing that the church, as a whole, is to act. This is a long-standing obligation which God has placed upon his people.

Questions
1. What are the prevailing sins of your city, town or village?
2. In what ways is your church in danger of being infected by attitudes and practices that are widely found outside its fellowship?
3. 'What business is it of mine to judge outsiders?' (12). What does Paul mean? Should we not criticize or speak out against the abuses and wrongs in society around us?

Church discipline

Should churches today imitate Paul's action, described in 5:5? Some churches have an elaborate system of discipline, with leaders exercising considerable power. Other churches do nothing, except pray, when members fall into sin. Opinions are divided about whether this is one of the ways in which we should imitate Paul, as he tells us in 4:16.

The factors we need to bear in mind when deciding this issue include the following:

- Paul believed that the whole Corinthian church had gone astray, not just the adulterer: see 5:2! The church thought there was nothing wrong. This affects Paul's response.

- Though Paul tells the Corinthians what to do, the action was to be taken by the whole church, and not just by the church leaders.

- In spite of 4:16, there are some ways in which, as an apostle, Paul could do things which we cannot. See the strange things he says about his spiritual presence in verses 3–4. It is possible that 'handing over to Satan' (5) is something that he alone could do.

- On the other hand, 5:11 is a clear instruction directed at all of us. The point is that *fellowship is impossible, when a fellow Christian is holding on to sinful practices in his or her life, and is unwilling to repent.* In such cases, Paul tells us to apply the principle expressed in Deuteronomy 17:7.

- In applying this principle, we will want to keep in mind the supreme aim of restoration, expressed in 5:5. Our actions must make it *more* likely, rather than *less* likely, that the sinner will be restored.

See Matthew 18:12–17 for Jesus' teaching on this.

1 Corinthians 6:1–11
Living as citizens of God's kingdom

The Corinthians were quick to take one another to court. Paul shows them that this is wrong and calls them to live consistent Christian lives instead.

 The inhabitants of ancient Greece were a people who took great delight in good lawsuits. Bearing in mind that a jury could sometimes have hundreds or even thousands of members, it is easy to see that virtually every Greek could think of himself as a lawyer! It is also easy to understand how, in such a culture, lawsuits were so popular.

The Corinthians had lived in this environment all their lives and it is scarcely surprising that within the church there were members who were running off to the law-courts and starting lawsuits against one another (1).

Yet though such conduct was, in one sense, not surprising, Paul is outraged. 'How dare you!' he roars!

He offers a number of reasons for his response. Surely, he says, if you must enter into such disputes it ought to be possible for you to resolve your difficulties within the church. After all, the Jews had always felt that disputes among themselves were best handled by their own number. Christianity, newly emerged from Judaism, ought to do the same.

Christians will be called to judge the world

However, there existed for Paul a far more important reason (2). For the apostle, what people believed should affect what they did. His own theology was especially dominated by 'eschatology', beliefs about the final hope that Christians all have.

Paul appeals to a truth with which the Corinthians were familiar (invariably when Paul says 'Don't you know?' he is appealing to received and widely circulated truth). At the end of the present age and in the world to come Christians will be given the highest dignity and will reign together with Jesus. As such they will even have authority over angels (3), the highest form of created beings. If such honour will be given to them then, it follows that the Corinthians ought to show themselves capable of dealing with the disputes, trifling by contrast, that were at present involving their members.

The exact meaning of Paul's words in verse 4 is not clear (compare the different translations of the Bible). However, he probably intends to show the absurdity of going to non-Christians, who do not enjoy the status and high calling of church members, to resolve disputes. This point is reinforced with a sharp sword-like cut (5). The Corinthians had made much of being 'wise', a fact that Paul has already had cause to challenge. If that is the case, he says, surely there must be somebody among you who can sort out your disputes!

In reality, however, and to the shame of the church in Corinth, all its dirty washing was dragged out and displayed for the unbelieving world to see (6). The Corinthians are seen to conduct themselves just like the unbelieving world and even below the standards of the more enlightened. They seem blind to the effects of their actions upon the church's witness and, more seriously, fail to apply received truths to their lives.

Christians must beware of being judged themselves

Paul has, however, left his greatest challenge till last. There was certainly a better way of resolving disputes within the congregation than going to law. But the mere fact that these disputes arose at all showed that the members of the church were still thinking in an ungodly and un-redeemed way. Selfishness and materialism dominated those who in-flicted injury: defence of personal rights was paramount to the wounded party (7, 8).

Wrong in themselves, such attitudes should have been completely out of place within the family of the church where loving concern and responsibility to others ought to have been the motivating factors.

Bluntly, Paul reaches his conclusion. Sin is sin and, persisted in and unrepented of, it is conduct that will bar its practitioner from the presence of God (9, 10).

The list of sins which Paul includes at this point shows, once again, the evil environment in which the Corinthians had lived and into which some, at least, had sunk (and were sinking again!). He points to several prevailing Corinthian sins which may well have lain behind the lawsuits (thieves, slanderers, swindlers). Others are touched on in 5:1–13; 6:12–20.

Note this (11)! While it was true that such sins were rife in Corinth, the gospel had demonstrated that the iron grip and influence of such things could be utterly broken. So, with that touch typical of Paul, this section ends on a high note! God the Father, through the empowering Spirit and on the basis of the redeeming work of Jesus Christ (note the almost unconscious way Paul introduces the Trinity), had brought cleansing, renewal and a fresh standing to those who had received the Christian message; a work effective in even the most dissipated.

The implication is clear: live as the people you are in Christ!

Questions
1. 'Why not rather submit to wrong?' (7). Should Christians never stand up for their rights in an unjust world?
2. What do you think Paul means by 'sexual pervert' (verse 9)? Would he include a stable homosexual relationship?
3. Can you think of examples in which the Christian message has been undermined by believers hanging out their dirty washing in public?

Christians and courts of law

The twin dangers of trivializing Paul's words or of making them apply to every situation need to be avoided here!

On the one hand we must not evade the very real challenge to church life that is contained in this passage by arguing that Paul was simply addressing a one-off situation in the Corinthian church.

On the other hand Paul does deal with the specific context of the life of the Corinthian congregation. He does not forbid all going to law (he did so himself on a number of occasions). This passage does not forbid our seeking legal advice and counsel in, for example, a house conveyance between believers.

What concerns Paul is the scandal of Christians who cannot agree seeking outside advice rather than resolving their problems within the family. Behind these actions are attitudes which so often divide a fellowship (whether or not they come to a legal action).

1 Corinthians 6:12–20
Our bodies are important to God

The Corinthians thought themselves so spiritual that it didn't matter what they did with their bodies. Paul replies by stressing how important our bodies really are.

During his ministry in Corinth Paul had probably sometimes used the phrase, *Everything is permissible for me* (12). Doubtless he had said these words when he was discussing Christian freedom where God had not specifically revealed his will. The phrase had been picked up by some of the Christians at Corinth and used as a slogan to justify their indulgence in acts of sin. The word translated 'permissible' occurs sixteen times in some form or another in the coming chapters. Once again, this had been reported to Paul and he recognized that it was vitally important to nip this error in the bud.

Paul does not attack the issue head on. He begins by indicating that the slogan cannot be universally applied. Is freedom always beneficial? Surely Christian freedom must never damage others. This, of course, cut to the heart of the Corinthian problem. Their whole theology and practice had self at the centre and asserted absolute personal freedom over against the needs and concerns of others.

Freedom can lead to bondage

But this was not all! Wisely Paul notes that the pursuit of freedom for freedom's sake can itself lead into a greater bondage (13). The 'freedom' to pursue a career, money, sex, or whatever else often leads a person into a far greater bondage than they had ever encountered before, because success in these areas is so demanding. Freedom is, therefore, to be used wisely and within the will of God.

This leads the apostle to the specific problem that he wished to address. He introduces it with another Corinthian slogan, *Food for the stomach and the stomach for food* (13). The Corinthians were extending this idea to include 'Sex for the body and the body for sex'. This would have been a quite natural point for the Corinthians to make, since ancient Greek culture did not tend to view sexual immorality as sinful.

However, it leads Paul to make some profound observations about the importance of the body. It is true, he says, that in the age to come there will be no place for stomachs because there will be no place for food. Certain bodily functions may end at death but the purpose of the body in its resurrection life continues; it lies within the scope of Christ's saving work (14).

It was always difficult to have a positive view of the body in the Greek-speaking world because Greek thought considered the body to be merely the prison of the soul. This view influenced the Corinthians but it is not the truth from God's point of view. The Old Testament sees each person as a body/soul – the body cannot be split off and treated as a separate thing. So Paul offers another slogan of his own: *The body is ... for the Lord and the Lord for the body*, and this fact rules out the use of the body for immoral, God-dishonouring purposes.

Now Paul again looks to the future. God has a purpose for the body which is permanent and extends into the age to come when it will be resurrected (see chapter 15). Not only were the Corinthians wrong to use the body in ways which were not God's will but they had lost sight of the lasting value which God has placed on the body. On two separate counts their application of their slogan to sexual immorality was incorrect.

Union with Christ leads to true freedom

There is more. At the root of the Christian gospel is the belief that through faith we have a real union with Jesus (15). Through faith-union our bodies become part of Christ's body. Consequently it is outrageous and sinful to unite his body, by a sinful act, with a prostitute (or 'available' housewife, secretary, *etc.*).

In case the Corinthians should dismiss his views as merely his own opinion, Paul offers scriptural support, appealing to Genesis 2:24 (16, 17). In Genesis it teaches that a real physical union is involved in the sexual act. If therefore the body of the believer is united (spiritually) to the Lord it is impossible for another competing and sinful union to be engaged in.

The application is bluntly made by the apostle in verse 18: sexual immorality is not something with which Christians can trifle; it must be resolutely rejected. The Corinthians probably used another slogan, 'all sin is outside the body', to excuse their indulgence. Perhaps so, says Paul, but sexual immorality is by no means 'outside the body'; it is a radical misuse of the body.

Paul's final point builds on this truth (19, 20): to defile the body, which is no mere shell for the soul but the sacred home of the Holy Spirit (of whom the Corinthians spoke so much!), is both utterly foolish and treasonable. For that very Spirit has been received as a result of Christ's purchase of the believer's body for himself. Since the purchaser has rights over his purchase, God has rights over the body of believers and it is his desire that the body be honoured, not dishonoured through defiling activity.

Paul's words in this section clearly have a significance beyond the church in Corinth. Not only does he establish the utter inappropriateness of sexual immorality; he also shows the honour with which our human bodies are invested by God. This is a dynamic understanding of what it means to be a Christian which is all too easily overlooked.

Questions
1. Is it true that 'Everything is permissible for me' (12)? Why does Paul say this (see 3:21–23 and 10: 23 – 11:1)?
2. In which part of the body do you think the Holy Spirit lives?
3. How might the Christian view of marriage be presented positively in today's world?

MARRIAGE AND DIVORCE
1 Corinthians 7:1–40

1 Corinthians 7:1–6

Is sex sinful?

Christians often have confused ideas about sex. This is no new problem. Paul here begins to tackle some of the faulty opinions found within the Corinthian church.

The church at Corinth, like many churches today, included people with a wide range of temperaments and beliefs. This explains why Paul can suddenly change from dealing with those who did not take sin seriously enough (chapters 5, 6) to those who tended to see sin where none existed!

Some of the Corinthian Christians clearly had problems with sex. They believed that the sexual act was in some way defiling and thought that the best possible course of action was to avoid the entanglements of marriage (or to escape from them where possible). They even thought it advisable not to touch the other sex because this was polluting (1). Paul literally says, 'It is good that a man does not touch a woman.' These are not Paul's words. Rather, as on a number of occasions in this letter, the apostle is quoting from the letter which the Corinthians had sent to him. We might paraphrase the verse, 'Now concerning the matters you wrote about, you report that some of your number say that it is good for a man not even to touch a woman.'

Paul does not immediately deny this claim. Wisely he seeks to undermine in a more subtle way the views of those who believed such things. He begins by making a practical observation (2). He reminds the Corinthian readers of where they are living and what their own temperaments are like. 'You', he says, 'are in a world where the temptations to sinful thought and action in the matter of sex are all around you. You, too, have natural drives which are aroused by such an environment. Consequently, marriage is of great benefit in meeting those desires in a legitimate way and so easing the temptation.'

We must not misunderstand Paul here. He is not saying that this is the only or even the main reason for marriage. Some have thought that this is what the apostle means and have condemned his views. Paul is not trying to give a complete statement about marriage. He is making one simple point: marriage does serve as a help when seeking to avoid sexual temptation.

Interestingly the word 'should have' is almost a command. Far from trying to avoid marriage, the Corinthians are encouraged to contract some! Some Corinthians who were married had apparently adopted the views of this anti-marriage group. They believed that while it was permissible to be married they were to abstain from sex. Paul will have none of this (3)! He stresses forcefully that the partners in a marriage have a moral duty to provide sexual satisfaction for one another. This would have staggered Paul's original readers. Far from suggesting that sex is defiling, he teaches that God's moral will is that marriage partners fulfil their obligations to one another in sexual union. Paul thus teaches that sexual union is (unless age or infirmity intervenes) an indispensable part of marriage (4). Moreover, these obligations apply equally to both partners.

Thus, says Paul, there can be only one possible ground for abstaining from sex in marriage (5). A married couple may temporarily abstain from sex when, by mutual agreement, they want to concentrate for a while on prayer. But it must be temporary, for long separation can result in strong temptation. Significantly, the word 'except' is a very hesitant word in the Greek in which Paul wrote. It is almost as though he says, 'Some of you weak brothers and sisters may find that sexual union hinders your spiritual exercises. If that is the case then the advice I offer you here is to be adopted.' For those without the scruples that these Corinthians had, there would seem, to the apostle, no possible reason ever to abstain from sex. Paul tries to emphasize this: 'I will make this concession to those who have scruples among you,' he says (6).

Questions
If you are studying this in a group, it might be appropriate to divide into marrieds and non-marrieds for the discussion. You will need to know each other well in order to talk this passage through. If fellowship is to be real then it ought to be possible to cope with talking about sex in a mixed group.

For marrieds
1. Is sex a right or a duty? How does Paul's teaching apply to couples where each partner's sex drive differs?
2. What advice do you think Paul would give to couples whose sex life has faded because of the pressures and busyness of life?

For singles
Paul himself was not married. Look ahead to verses 7–9 for his specific comments about singleness. How can you tell whether singleness is your 'gift'?

For all
Western society is sex-obsessed. How can Christians be a positive witness in such a culture?

1 Corinthians 7:7–16
Singleness and marriage: which is better?

Many Corinthian Christians were still confused over issues of singleness and marriage and the spiritual effects of being married to an unbeliever. Paul answers these difficult questions.

Paul, of course, was probably now a single man who had presumably been widowed (he would not have been allowed to obtain the high standing he had among the Jews before his conversion if he had been unmarried). He, himself, no longer experienced strong enticement to sexual sin. He realized that this was a spiritual gift (*charisma*) from God and had certain advantages (as we shall see in verses 26ff.). But he also realized that if a life of singleness is a gift from God so is marriage: *one has this gift, another has that* (7). These opposite courses of action are equally correct and honouring to God, depending as they do upon his gift.

Such general teaching is followed by practical advice and application (8). All those who are not at present married (whether single, divorced or, especially, the vulnerable widowed) are encouraged to see that there may be good grounds to remain as they are. These are not detailed here but see, again, verses 26ff. However, their decision is to be based on what is best for them and on God's gifting, not because there is something morally superior about singleness. Moreover, the decision to remain single may be changed later. Paul implies this by the use of a phrase which cannot be translated into English. He seems to mean, 'It is good for them to decide to remain single at present'. Where, however, the temptation is great it is clearly better to marry than to suffer the distraction of aroused passion (9).

Some, however, in Corinth had clearly gone so far as to renounce their marriage vows because of their views about sex. Paul thunders at them! If, so far, he had offered his opinion as an apostle, he now gives a *command*: the will of the Lord Jesus. He refers to the words recorded in Matthew 5:31, 32 and 19:1–12 (10). Marriage is an indissoluble bond, so the possibility of divorcing one's partner on the basis that sex is defiling is completely invalid (11).

Others, of course, might have used such grounds to escape from an unhappy marriage. This Paul rejects. Separation may be a less-than-acceptable possibility in such circumstances but divorce is entirely ruled out. The apostle counsels reconciliation.

Mixed-faith marriages

So far Paul has discussed marriages between Christians. But what happens when only one of the partners in a marriage is converted? Paul offers his opinion as an apostle. Where the unbeliever remains happy to live with the believer the marriage is to be sustained. The Christian is forbidden to seek divorce (12, 13).

Paul's verdict here would doubtless have disturbed some of his readers. 'After all', some would have reasoned, 'even if sex with a believing partner is all right, surely sex with an unbelieving partner is defiling. Moreover, what about children born to such a union: are they not impure?' But Paul reverses the argument in a manner strange to our ears but consistent with the way his readers reasoned. 'It is not that the good is polluted by the bad but the bad is made acceptable by the good,' says Paul. 'So you need have no anxiety about your children, and your marriage need not be dissolved' (14).

However, in a church where all the members were recent converts, another problem could arise if the unbelieving partner found it intolerable to live with the converted spouse. If the unbeliever sought a divorce, what should the believer do? Paul shows his pastoral heart here as he seeks to deal tenderly with those caught up in such a situation. A biblical principle is that marriage is not to be dissolved. But another biblical principle is that of peace and this may sometimes have precedence. Thus, divorce is permitted where the believer does not take the initiative. It would also appear that remarriage is considered as possible: for 'not bound' reflects legal language which implied the right of remarriage (15).

There is, however, a balancing truth to be borne in mind. To remain with an unbelieving partner is to stay in a situation where there is at least a possibility of seeing the salvation of the other (16). The chance of achieving the other's salvation is to be kept firmly in view.

Questions

You will need to be especially sensitive in the group as you discuss these questions.

1. Do I recognize my present single or marital state as a gift from God (see verse 7)?
2. How could our churches minister (more) effectively to members with non-Christian husbands or wives?
3. How might we encourage non-Christians to recognize the wisdom of God's attitude to marriage?
4. Is divorce wrong? Is remarriage after divorce wrong? Set Paul's teaching alongside that of Jesus in Matthew 19:3–12. Are they teaching the same thing?

Divorce and remarriage

Broadly speaking there are three different ways in which the reader can understand Paul's teaching in this chapter and in the light of Scripture as a whole.

1. Jesus taught that divorce is permissible only where adultery has taken place (*e.g.*, Matthew 19:1–12). Remarriage is possible for the innocent party. Paul is then considered to add a further ground (desertion) or thought to teach that separation but not divorce is possible where a spouse is abandoned. Moses' teaching (Deuteronomy 24:1–4) is considered to be replaced by Jesus' teaching.

2. The second view similarly allows separation for both adultery and desertion but (on the basis of verse 39 of this chapter) denies any right to remarriage during the lifetime of the former partner.

3. The third view is that adopted here. Divorce is always less than the best (Jesus' point) but is possible for a range of (ultimately unspecified) causes (as Moses realized and Paul affirms). However, where divorce has taken place, remarriage is permissible, although not always advisable. Thus, Jesus dealt with the ideal, Moses and Paul with pastoral realities. It is important that due emphasis is given to both these aspects of biblical teaching.

For further reading see the end of this book.

1 Corinthians 7:17–40
Problems in following God's call

Christians often have to face difficult life choices, especially concerning marriage. Paul recognizes the complex questions that do arise and here offers some guidance in handling them.

What effect does conversion to Christ have on a person's social situation? A believer, says Paul, should remain content with that state of life which was his or hers at conversion. Conversion will make a radical difference to one's spiritual and moral life, but it may not change one's outward life and circumstances at all and believers are not to become restless (17). Paul takes circumcision as an example (18). Those who were circumcised were not to be ashamed and try and conceal the mark. Equally, the uncircumcised were not to become restless for circumcision. Of far greater importance was the general obedience of the believer to God (19). The gospel of Jesus and its blessings can be enjoyed in all their fullness in every situation of life: outward circumstances are not important when a life is lived to the glory of God (20).

Paul concludes with an outrageous example (21)! Both religious and social divisions are unimportant. Even a slave can live to the honour of God just as well as someone who is free. No doubt a slave should take his freedom if the chance is offered, but if he were free he would not necessarily be better able to honour God. Rather, a Christian remains called by the Lord whatever he is or does. He has been freed from sin to serve the Lord: that is what counts. The slave is, of course, to obey God rather than man when there is a conflict; however, the basic principle of being content with one's station in life still stands (22–24).

The question of singleness
The Corinthians had clearly asked Paul a number of questions concern-

84

ing singleness and marriage. *Now about virgins* refers to one of them (25). The question seem to have been this: 'Should an engaged girl go ahead with marriage in the normal way?' Paul says that this was a matter upon which Jesus had never spoken (compare verse 12). Moreover, he makes no appeal here to his apostolic authority (see verse 17). Rather, he only offers his opinion, though he thinks his views are worthy of respect.

Once again the apostle alludes to the Corinthians' letter (26). They had said, 'A single person is wise if he or she does not marry.' Paul, however, emphasizes that this may be true in some circumstances but singleness is in no way superior to marriage in general (26).

But what does Paul mean when he speaks of 'the present (or impending) distress'? He is probably referring to those difficulties which were predicted to occur during the early days of the Christian church or to some difficulty which the Corinthian church was already going through: persecution of some sort. His point, then, is simply this: 'You are at present (or soon will be) experiencing considerable stress as a result of persecution. Now, a married woman, especially one with a young family, is going to be under great pressure and anxiety, fearing for her husband and children. This can be avoided by remaining single. At the present time it may, therefore, be wise to remain single.' Paul's advice would doubtless have been different at a more peaceful time.

So although married people had no grounds for divorce in the idea that there was something sinful about sex, persecution might make it expedient to remain single. Paul repeats his point in verse 28 in case his readers have failed to notice it.

Like many a preacher, Paul is reluctant to leave his subject until he feels quite sure no-one has missed what he is saying (29)! So, using language drawn from the final suffering and end of the world, he makes the point that the institutions of the world are not permanent. Thus, Christians are to seek to live without undue regard for them (30, 31).

But this is easier said than done! Paul knows this and so repeats his point that the single person is relatively free from care in such circumstances (32). He does not mean here that *in general* the married person cannot be as devoted to the Lord as the single person. This would mean that Paul had fallen into the same trap as the Corinthians. Paul never admits that either marriage or singleness is better than the other. He does recognize that sometimes singleness is desirable. The obligations arising from marriage may give a persecuted believer great distress (33–34), which can be escaped by remaining single and having only the Lord to think about (35). Under different circumstances we must suppose that Paul would have commended marriage over against singleness. So, for

85

example, many Christian workers find that marriage helps them more fully to serve the Lord since there is someone with whom the load can be shared and who is able to offer a degree of support, encouragement, care and protection which is necessary to fulfil their ministries.

Fathers and daughters

The meaning of verses 36–38 is not at all clear. They could refer to the father of a woman or the fiancé of a girl. The NIV includes the former in the margin and the latter in the text. A third possibility is that Paul is describing a kind of 'spiritual marriage' in which the virgin remains unmarried but lives in a mixed community. The authors marginally favour the reference as being to a father and engaged daughter. However, the application of the principles to our own situation is clear enough whichever Paul meant!

What should a father do about his engaged daughter? Should he allow her to marry or not? Paul offers his advice and, once again, emphasizes that the decision is not to be taken because of any supposed sinfulness which attends marriage and sex. Rather, a wise consideration of all the circumstances is required. For example, the girl's age needs to be taken into account. If she is still young the present difficulties might favour the refusal of marriage. However, if she is older and the chances of security for the future which marriage brings are receding, it might be more appropriate to allow her to marry. Her future security may be more important than the present difficulties. In the Corinthians' present circumstances singleness is generally preferable but the person who, on the basis of other considerations, agrees to marriage neither sins nor acts in a way that is less spiritual.

Should widows remarry?

It would appear that the Corinthians asked Paul one last question on the subject: 'Should widows remarry?' We can understand that those with scruples about sex might well think sexual relations with another's spouse as in some way defiling. Paul's answer is simple and consistent with everything that he has said in this chapter. Death brings a marriage contract to an end. Nothing then stands in the way of remarriage. Again, however, in the light of the present situation facing the church, remaining single may prove the better option (39, 40).

We must not misunderstand Paul's words. He does not discuss other possible situations, for example divorce. It is not fair to take Paul's words, as some have, and suggest that a divorcee cannot remarry until the former spouse is dead. Paul does not say this, so neither should we!

Questions
1. Do I take important decisions in my life as seriously as I should? Am I ready to sacrifice my own desires for the sake of the Lord?
2. How might Paul's teaching help the church address some of the complex issues concerning marriage which face society today? For instance, do children always benefit from father and mother staying together 'for their sake'? When divorcees, both with children, marry each other, how can the children be helped to accept each other?

When Christians disagree

The interpretation taken in this chapter is not agreed by all Christians, as has been indicated in 'Divorce and remarriage' (p. 83). Careful consideration ought to be given to such views. However, limitations of space have permitted the presentation of only one view within the context of the explanation of this difficult chapter.

There is, however, a lesson to learn from this! Sometimes Christians conscientiously disagree in their understanding of a passage of Scripture. We need to be aware of this and charitable to those who disagree with us when certainty is difficult.

CHRISTIANS IN PAGAN SOCIETY
1 Corinthians 8:1 – 11:1

1 Corinthians 8:1–13

Living in love

Some members of the Corinthian church considered themselves to be strong and disregarded the scruples and needs of others. Paul rebukes them; the absence of love in their dealing with others is damning!

Paul has begun to work through some of the issues the Corinthian church had written to him about. He now turns to a matter which obviously figured largely in the correspondence, since his reply occupies 8:1 – 11:1. The issue is the eating of food sacrificed to idols.

It would have been impossible to have escaped this issue in ancient Corinth (see 'Meat sacrificed to idols': p. 93); it was obviously a matter widely debated in the Corinthian congregation and no agreement had been reached.

Paul refers to their question (1) only to appear to go off at a complete tangent and refer to knowledge! However, that was the essential problem; there were those in the congregation who felt that they had 'knowledge' which enabled them to attend pagan feasts with impunity. Paul does not necessarily deny their claims, but argues that there were other considerations which they were ignoring.

Simply put, knowledge which is attained and applied without loving concern leads to self-assertion and pride, which often ride roughshod over the needs of others. For the apostle this is a vital point; the aim of Christian teaching and action is the meeting of the needs of others.

Paul turns to those who proudly claimed 'knowledge' in the area of food sacrificed to idols. Such boasts, he says, indicate that there is a vital ingredient missing (2). In fact, without the evidence of love for God (seen in loving concern for others), it has to be asked whether the claim to be known by God is true (3).

Paul now proceeds to the specific issue (4). He begins by apparently quoting from the letter he had received and agreeing with the two points that the letter had made; that there is only one God and, therefore, the 'gods' worshipped in pagan ceremonies did not really exist. On the basis of this, some of the Corinthians felt free to go to meals at pagan shrines.

The details of verses 5 and 6 have troubled commentators and translators alike; hence the differences between translations of the Bible. However, the overall sense is clear enough. It is possible that Paul is quoting again from the Corinthians' letter and he is agreeing with their fundamental point. It is true, he says, that many different 'gods' are worshipped; both the 'gods' of the traditional cults and the 'lords' of some of the newer 'mystery' religions. However, for the believer ('us') there ought to be the recognition that there really was no other God than the Christian one.

This claim is accompanied by an almost creed-like statement which, however, appears to have been created by Paul for the occasion. It will become clear that the apostle wishes to establish his teaching on the basis of what the church confesses.

For Paul Christian teaching is not merely a standard of orthodoxy but the basis of all Christian conduct. Within the one God there exist, he says, both the Father and the Lord Jesus Christ. The Father is the creator and the object of all true service. The Lord Jesus was the one through whom the world was made and the one through whom every believer has experienced spiritual life. This being so, the apostle goes on to point out the fundamental weakness of the views of those believers who asserted their freedom to go to pagan feasts.

Recent (and not so recent) converts still struggle with Christian truths and how to work them out in their lives. Even though they have been well taught, they find it difficult to escape patterns of thinking that dominated them prior to their conversion. What is true today was also a problem in Paul's time (7).

In the light of this, Paul teaches that not every member of the Corinthian congregation had come to the same secure understanding of the truth as those whose views had been quoted in the letter. When such people attend gatherings where sacrifices were offered to pagan gods they were troubled, unable to free themselves from, especially, those inner (even irrational) emotions which still persuaded them there was some reality to the ceremonies and the gods they honoured. Indeed, real Satanic power may well have been connected with temple worship, so the fears of the scrupulous were not only 'in the mind'.

The result of all this was that they were 'defiled', led into a form of idolatry. This conclusion remains true, Paul says, even though the 'strong' believers' slogan was true, *Food does not bring us near to God; we are no worse if we do not eat, and no better if we do* (8).

The Corinthians claimed that they had the right to exercise their freedom in accordance with their knowledge. Paul does not deny their theology or their freedom but he does deny their emphasis upon personal rights. The exercise of freedom may, in fact, prove a hindrance to the faith of another Christian (9).

The believer who still has scruples about meals in pagan temples may be encouraged to attend such gatherings if he sees other believers doing so. So he will believe that he is doing something (sacrificing to an idol) which is acceptable as a Christian (10, 11). However, such worship of other gods is wrong (it is idolatry) and he will, therefore, be drawn away from the true faith and be placed on the road which leads to destruction.

Tragically, all this will be the result of one believer insisting on his or her own freedoms in Christ; by the 'strong' flexing his or her own muscles at the expense of the 'weak'. But those very freedoms will have spiritually destroyed someone for whom Jesus died.

Such a situation is tragic in itself. But it is trebly sad because by acting in such a way the 'strong' believer will have also sinned both against the person he has destroyed and against the very one who died for him too! Freedom exercised irresponsibly and uncaringly is, Paul bluntly says, sin (12)!

So Christian freedom is to be limited by the needs of others and their upbuilding. If this means even permanently restricting oneself from exercising a legitimate freedom, then so be it. The brother (note how the word 'brother' occurs four times in this passage!) or sister is far more important than my freedoms and rights! Paul becomes quite passionate about it (13): *I will never eat meat again ...*

Questions
1. What are the 'gods' of this age which are still hampering my Christian growth? How can I get free from them?
2. What issues within the life of your fellowship can you list where it is possible to be right but where insistence on the right may harm others?
3. What do you think would strike non-Christians most if believers lived out the lessons of this chapter?

Meat sacrificed to idols

Eating meals in pagan temples was a regular part of worship in ancient Greece and occupied a significant place in the social life of the community. Even those who were not followers of the ancient cults would, nevertheless, frequently attend private or public social functions within pagan temples. Instead of a reception at a hotel, the Greeks would often hold a feast in a temple. The devout Greeks believed that at these meals, held in honour of the gods and where sacrifices were offered to them, the gods were actually present.

For many, Christians included, it would have been necessary for their livelihood to attend temple feasts held by their trade-guilds, feasts held in honour of the patron 'god' of their trade. A modern, but not exact, parallel might be the expectation that some should be Freemasons and attend Lodge meetings.

Usually the feast would have three parts. First there was the preparation, then the sacrifice and finally the feast. The meat of the sacrifice was divided into three; one part consumed in the sacrifice, another given to the worshippers and a part placed on the 'table of the gods'. The meat left over from such feasts was usually sold in the local market.

All this faced the new believer with a whole range of questions: for example, should meat which has been sacrificed to a god be purchased and eaten (and how can you tell whether it had been?) and was it all right to attend a feast in a pagan temple simply as a social function?

It is clear that these questions lie behind Paul's words in 8:1 – 11:1. The church was unable to come to a common view and had sought Paul's advice.

Other complicating factors may also have been involved. The Jews prohibited the eating of food sacrificed to idols because it was tainted with idolatry, the heathen had not tithed it and it had probably not been slaughtered in the proper way. Those influenced by a Jewish background would have thought these issues as important in the discussion. Then there was the Jerusalem decree (Acts 15:29), apparently only a temporary injunction upon the church, but still a recent decision by honoured leaders.

It was not surprising that this was a contentious issue. It required a clear understanding of God's truth and will to offer a satisfying reply to all the questions which were raised. Paul was on the spot!

1 Corinthians 9:1–14
The rights of Christian workers

Christian workers should be adequately supported with money and other material benefits because of the spiritual work that they do. But ministry is never about rights!

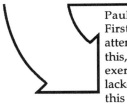 Paul was being challenged from two directions. First, some questioned his command forbidding attendance at meals in pagan temples. Linked with this, others were suggesting that his own failure to exercise freedom in this matter showed that he lacked the proper credentials to be an apostle. In this chapter he provides an answer to both these charges. He is both free and an apostle. However, as we shall see, the answer he gives cuts away to the heart the unspiritual attitudes of his questioners (1, 2).

The New Testament uses the word 'apostle' in a number of different ways. In this case Paul is probably defending his claim to be one of the unique foundation-stones of the Christian church through whom the Christian message was fully and finally revealed.

He appeals to his experience on the Damascus road where he had seen the resurrected Jesus and had been commissioned by him personally (Acts 9:1–19). However, he does not make a thorough defence of his claim. With a touch of sadness, he simply adds that the Corinthians themselves should have been the last people with doubts, since it was the establishing of their church which, for them, ought to have been evidence of his apostolic call.

As a theological argument his appeal is incomplete. But Paul is not concerned here to offer a full defence of his position as an apostle. Rather, he offers just enough to prick the consciences of the hardened members of the Corinthian church and show his sorrow that they could be so fickle and misguided in their attitudes toward him.

94

But this was not all! Their challenge was that he had failed to exercise freedom (3)! It was on his 'failure' here that their 'judgment' had taken place. Paul replies that as an apostle and Christian he had every right to eat and drink whatever he liked (even the food and drink that had been sacrificed to idols: 4).

They had also suggested that Paul ought to have exercised his freedom in other ways. 'Why is he not married?' they were asking, and, 'Why does he not seek support from us for his ministry but work for a living?' After all, others had lived in this way (5, 6).

Should Christian work be paid for?

In the Greek-speaking world it was generally believed that a philosopher or teacher ought to be paid for his work. Thus those, like Plato and Socrates, who taught freely were sometimes charged with offering teaching which couldn't amount to much if they didn't seek a fee. Manual tasks, however, were regarded (rather as they sometimes are today) as second-class within respectable Greek society. Then again, it was unusual (and slightly degrading) for a man to be unmarried in the ancient world.

To the Corinthians, obsessed by their belief that they were highly spiritual and that freedom was to be demonstrated in the exercise of power and authority, this was a considerable problem. Paul just was not living the lifestyle one would expect of a great leader and teacher.

In his response, Paul does not deny his right to these things. In fact he provides what amounts to the most comprehensive statement of the right of a Christian worker to adequate support that we find in the entire Bible! But, as we shall see, he had reasons which made him renounce such rights.

But if he renounced them it is quite another matter for the Christian community not to offer them (as indeed, to their credit, the Corinthians did).

Paul offers several reasons for his views. First of all he appeals to natural justice (8). Whether engaged in work for others, self-employed or even someone else's slave, it is usual to expect to be provided for and to benefit from any labour undertaken. The standards for the world at large ought not to be neglected by the church!

But to such human wisdom a further, and more compelling, reason is added. The Scriptures themselves require that God's people repay their workers adequately (8–10). Paul quotes from Deuteronomy 25:4 showing that it is the underlying principle which is intended to be grasped and applied. Since the verse in Deuteronomy actually occurs in the middle of a large number of social laws, perhaps it was always intended to be applied to human activities, not just to animals. But in any case the Jews always believed that 'the greater application was contained within the lesser'. Either way, therefore, workers have every reason to 'hope' for a wage.

Material support should be given to those engaged in spiritual activities (11, 12a). Paul here seems to reject the view (still too often found today) that spiritual 'work' ought to be accompanied by 'spiritual' rewards. This opinion has the 'merit' of appearing highly 'spiritual' while, often, excusing the person who suggests it from paying anything. But Paul argues that, at the very least, a Christian worker should have adequate financial support.

Two final reasons for supporting Christian workers clinch Paul's argument (12b–14). First, it was a widespread practice in the ancient world (and the practice was endorsed by Old Testament law) that those engaged in the service of God were rewarded. But more significantly Jesus had commanded the same practice for those engaged in Christian service (Luke 10:7).

The Corinthians had recognized this in the case of others. Why not also for Paul? He had every right to their support. But he was free: free to refuse it!

Questions

1. Are there ways that I could increase my practical support for Christian workers I know?
2. How does your church assess in a realistic way the financial needs of those for whom it is responsible?
3. Western missionaries in the Third World are often paid far more than the people they are working with. What would Paul say to them? Are some paid too little? If it is possible ask some missionaries for their views.
4. Paul had apparently given up marriage for the sake of the gospel (5). Should this be usual or only a rare pattern for Christian workers (see also 1 Corinthians 11:1)?
5. What do you think the unbelieving world might think if it was aware of the poor support many Christian workers are given?

1 Corinthians 9:15–27
Free to serve the gospel

The Corinthians thought freedom meant the opportunity to exercise power and authority. Paul teaches that true freedom is to become a servant of all for the sake of the gospel.

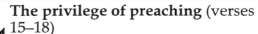

The privilege of preaching (verses 15–18)

Paul has established his right to be paid for preaching the gospel, but there are things that are (or ought to be) far more important to Christian workers than their 'rights'. To preach the gospel is such a privilege that financial gain fades into the background in comparison with the rewards of the job itself (16–17).

Preaching is certainly a privilege, but not a ground for personal pride because the preacher does not choose his or her calling; God does. No-one can be proud of simply doing what God has demanded of him or her under pain of judgment!

Paul asks the question, 'Under such circumstances can I speak of reward at all?' (18). His response is paradoxical. Such reward as I have, he says, is to renounce all rights and preach the gospel without charge. His reward is to have no reward, or, his reward is to go the extra mile, strain every sinew and do it all extravagantly well.

This idea is a world apart from the attitude of the Corinthians! For them freedom was the right of the Christian worker to demand his or her rights. For Paul, rights are swallowed up by the freedom to renounce these rights for the sake of the gospel.

This does not imply that everyone should refuse support but it does mean that this support must not be seen as something 'earned' or a reward for services rendered to God and his people. If the circumstances seem to require it, the Christian worker should freely renounce such 'rights' so that the gospel might not be compromised or so that its cause might be advanced.

The first part of verse 19 looks rather like a Corinthian slogan; true Christians enjoy freedom! Paul accepts this but not in quite the way the Corinthians understood it! For them it meant freedom to rule; for Paul it meant freedom to serve.

When to yield and when to be firm (verses 20–23)

Perhaps the Corinthians had accused Paul of inconsistency in the way that he related to the various groups he preached to. While he never altered the content of the gospel, he was always ready to meet people where they were, if the truth itself was not at stake. For him, the barriers of race, religion and conscience (indeed, all those things that divide men and women) were unimportant. Hence if it meant adopting a Jewish (or some other) way of life in order to make a bridge to others, he would be more than willing to do it. No-one was more yielding in unimportant matters than Paul, and none more unyielding where the gospel itself was at stake!

Paul here offers another paradox. In one way, he was free to become a servant. Yet, viewed in another light, he was bound to such conduct by the demands of both God and Christ. The reason for this was simple. He had been called by God to preach the gospel (see verse 16) and therefore he was obliged to sacrifice everything short of the truth itself so that men and women might be brought to a saving knowledge of God.

Paul obviously breathed a different air from the Corinthians. For all their claims to an exalted spirituality, to their freedom and authority in Christ, they were a people still dominated by worldly considerations and an emphasis upon personal rights.

Spiritual training (verses 24–27)

Paul now encourages the Corinthian believers to get down to the business of true discipleship. Using illustrations drawn from athletic contests, he shows that if dedication and effort are required to compete successfully, then it is all the more true in the spiritual realm.

The Isthmian Games (second only to the Olympic Games in their importance in ancient Greece) were held in the suburbs of Corinth every couple of years. Most Corinthians would have seen the games and observed the rigorous training which the athletes put themselves through in order to compete.

Paul's first point is that no prize is ever won without complete dedication and an absolute will to win. However, sheer willpower and dedication never won an athletic contest on its own. Rigorous and self-denying training is vital if ever a competitor is to compete successfully. Yet even this is not enough. The most successful athletes are those who have a specific target in view and whose training is dictated by this one goal. Even today athletes sometimes 'peak' too early or late to achieve success in the event which they had set their hearts on winning.

The wonder of all of this is that the reward is so fleeting. In the Isthmian Games the winner was rewarded with a pine wreath which soon withered and disintegrated. Today the medals won at major championships are no more that a piece of ribbon and plated metal, materials worth almost nothing.

This makes Paul's challenge to the Corinthians very pointed. Some of them at least had so persuaded themselves that they were already living the life of the age to come that the need for pressing on to the goal had been lost. Others felt that their spiritual gifts confirmed that they had arrived at perfection and no further effort was required.

But Paul will have none of this! The goal still lies ahead; a glorious goal which deserves every ounce of effort to obtain. And, until it is reached, single-minded dedication and rigorous training are required.

In all of this Paul was not requiring anything that he did not demand of himself (26, 27). When he ran, it was not aimless jogging. When he fought it was against real opposition. In fact he would go through the pain barrier if it served him and his goal. Everything – his rights, his authority, his freedom; all those things mentioned in this chapter – were to become subservient to his obligation to disciple men and women for Christ.

Paul here is not merely thinking of the body as sinful and requiring mortification. Sometimes even things good in themselves need to be set aside to gain the prize. But which prize might he miss? It is not obvious which prize he had in mind when he thought he might fail to win it. Nor is it clear whether he considered it a real possibility that he could miss it. Thus the wider theological questions that so often preoccupy discussion of this verse need to be set aside in favour of noting the way that Paul's language, in its context, stresses vividly the necessity of disciplined living for Christ.

Questions
1. Are there legitimate things that God is requiring me to give up for the sake of his calling upon my life?
2. Paul became 'all things to all people' to win them for Christ (22).

What sort of things should our church be doing to follow his example?

3. Do you think that non-Christians are impressed by Christians trying to win them by using worldly methods (such as loud music, persuasive advertising, threats, promises of rewards ...)?

1 Corinthians 10:1–13
The lessons of history

Paul shows the Corinthians that there are lessons to be drawn from God's past dealings with his people that they neglect at their peril.

 Throughout this section Paul has been struggling to reassert his authority over the Corinthian church, especially concerning their attendance at pagan temples. He has shown that the problem lies at a far deeper level than his opponents realized. They had a completely different view of the 'normal Christian life'.

In 9:24–27, Paul therefore emphasized that Christian living requires self-sacrifice, studied effort and a steady aim. In chapter 10 he shows that this is a challenge that all who claim to be disciples of Jesus must take up. He uses an illustration from the Old Testament. Paul, the apostle of the Gentiles (or non-Jews), argues that the New Testament church comprises the true descendants of the Old Testament people of God. So, in appealing to the stories of Israel in the wilderness, he can speak of 'our forefathers' (1).

He then shows how these stories have a relevance to his readers (2). The Israelites had been blessed by God in a quite remarkable way. Though they passed through the Red Sea on dry ground, yet there was a real parallel between their experience and the Christian who passes through the waters of baptism. The Christian, too, enjoys the presence of God, just as the Israelites experienced the nearness of God in the cloud. And just as these experiences united the Israelites around Moses, their leader, so the Christian is, through baptism, united to Jesus.

Moreover, just as the Christian enjoys the continuing strengthening of his or her spiritual life through holy communion, so the Israelites were supplied with 'spiritual' food and drink to sustain them, an experience which continued throughout all their journeys through the wilderness (3, 4).

Nevertheless, though 'they all' (notice how this phrase is repeated throughout verses 1–4) experienced these things, they were found to be displeasing to God, the wilderness was scattered with their dead bodies and only a few (in fact only two!) entered into the land which God had promised his people (5).

At this point, too, there was a parallel between what happened to them and the Corinthian church (6). Indeed, as Paul points out, the events of the wilderness could scarcely be much of a lesson to dead people, but are recorded in the Old Testament Scriptures so that those who followed might learn from the past and not fall into the mistakes of earlier generations.

Idolatry today?

Gradually it becomes clear why Paul has used this part of the Old Testament story. The snare into which the Israelites fell was idolatry (7). Interestingly, the story (recorded in Exodus 32) suggests that the people themselves did not consider what they did idolatrous; they were merely making an image of their God and devising their own way of worshipping him. However, the verdict of the Old Testament is clear: it was idolatry and, like so much idolatry, it became the means by which they were led into sexual immorality.

In verses 7–10 Paul makes clear the four aspects of the Israelites' wrongdoing and expects his Corinthian readers to take the point:

- idolatry and pagan revelry (verse 7)

- sexual immorality (verse 8)

- testing the Lord (verse 9)

- grumbling (verse 10).

These were the very temptations faced by those Christians who attended pagan feasts. The Corinthians thought that they were 'protected' by the fact that they had been baptized and continued to meet around the communion table. However, this did not mean they could freely enter pagan temples and take part in the activities which took place there, including prostitution (8). This was to mix the true worship of God with pagan worship, just as the Israelites had done in the wilderness. And if the Israelites suffered the wrath of God as a result, the warning to the Corinthians was clear enough!

The Israelites had tested God by complaining against the leader whom God had given them. The result was tragic (9, 10)!

So Paul warns the freedom-loving Corinthians who resisted his apostolic authority, especially those insisting that they could attend functions in pagan temples (11). Just as the judgment of God followed the Israelites' disobedience, so, he implies, they stand under the coming judgment of God if they persist in such practices.

And should the Corinthians be tempted to dismiss his illustration as 'merely from the Old Testament', Paul is quick to point out that the whole of the Old Testament Scriptures find their fulfilment in the Christian era. If, therefore, God's judgment accompanied the idolatry of his people in earlier times, it could not be less the case at the time Paul wrote (12)!

God has never promised protection to those believers who deliberately place themselves where temptation is inevitable and avoidable. However, where God's children seek to follow him faithfully, he does guarantee his protection (13).

Perhaps Paul was addressing a specific worry that some Corinthians may have felt. They may have been attending pagan festivals because they feared the social consequences that might follow. After all, such festivals would have been seen in Corinth as a harmless custom. If this is the case, Paul does not promise that they will not have to face many difficulties and tests to their faith; he does, however, guarantee that God will sustain his children even in the darkest hour.

Verse 13 has been a great comfort and strength to countless Christians since Paul wrote it. It is a promise to cherish.

Questions
1. Paul teaches that 'grumbling' can seriously damage our eternal health (10). What does it involve? Why is it so serious?
2. In what ways might our congregation be in danger of idolatry? Is it possible to treat God himself as an idol if we have wrong ideas about him?
3. What idols are to be found in modern society? How do they influence us?

Paul's use of the Old Testament

Paul offers us here a very good example of how to benefit from reading the Old Testament stories. His starting point is that God does not change in the way that he deals with his people (and his people don't change much either!). This means that when we read stories of long ago, we are to recognize that the same dangers and snares beset us and the same encouragements and warnings are to be applied to us.

On the detailed way in which Paul uses the Old Testament in this passage it is necessary to consult more scholarly works.

Does baptism save and can the saved be lost?

It is possible to read Paul's words here and conclude that he believes the sacraments (baptism and holy communion) actually save the person who takes part in them. This is not, however, what Paul means.

In New Testament times baptism was seen as the visible way in which a person responded to the Christian message. So baptism almost always seems to have occurred as soon as faith was professed (for example, see Acts 2:41).

Because faith and baptism were so closely linked, it was possible (as here) to speak of the one in place of the other. If Paul had been offering a full statement here he would probably have said that 'faith expressed in baptism saves'. Our problem is that we usually split baptism off from the initial response of faith. Paul suggests that the sacraments nourish faith and faith is expressed in the sacraments.

It is easy to appeal to this passage as evidence that the saved can be lost; easy, but incorrect. Paul is not dealing with wider theological issues here but simply stating that those who persist in rebellion against God, whatever their 'Christian' credentials, place themselves under the judgment of God. It is not those who say they are believers but those who live as believers that God approves. Wider theological questions must be resolved elsewhere.

1 Corinthians 10:14 – 11:1
Right and wrong!

Knowing God's will for us is not always easy. Here Paul offers some basic advice to help us make the right choices.

The discussion which began at 8:1 concludes with this section. It has not been easy for Paul to tackle the issue as to whether or not it was right for Christians to attend pagan temples, for the temperature ran high between him and some of the Corinthians. It says much for the apostle's greatness, therefore, that despite the disagreements he could still address them as 'dear friends' (14).

In the two short paragraphs which follow (10:14–22; 10:23 – 11:1) he concludes by offering some sound advice to the Corinthians, based on his previous discussion.

Common sense and Scripture

His first point is that there are occasions when decision-making is really quite easy (14–15); idolatry and Christianity never mix! This, Paul argues, needs no proof; sometimes a good dose of common sense is all that is required to determine God's will! But Paul does not rely merely on common sense; good theology establishes the same point (16, 17)!

Paul reminds his readers of the truths that they had been taught about the Lord's Supper. Sharing a meal in the ancient world was an expression of fellowship. Paul picks up this familiar picture here and applies it to communion. When Christians meet together around the Lord's Table then, in so doing, they declare and enjoy fellowship with one another and (more remarkable still) with God himself; they are 'partners' together. This was true of times even more ancient than Paul's day. Appealing to Deuteronomy 14:22–27, Paul shows that those who shared a sacrificial meal were bound together in common fellowship with God (18).

Now he answers a possible objection (19). It is quite probable that the Corinthians justified their conduct by appealing to their faith that there was only one true God. Paul agrees, of course, but suggests that false religion is often inspired (even empowered) by deceiving demonic forces (20). The last thing that Paul would wish was for anyone to come under the influence of demonic powers.

There is also a 'logical' problem. It is impossible for someone to be an intimate friend with both of such sworn enemies. It is impossible to sit on the fence. God's jealousy for his own unique glory cannot be challenged. If we try to mix worship of God with other beings or things it will be to our cost.

How to discover God's will for us

There are, of course, other situations where the decision is less easy to make. There are many things that God has not specifically forbidden. The Corinthians had, therefore, come up with a slogan to express their belief that they were free to do anything God had not denied to them; '*Everything is permissible*,' they cried (23).

Typically, Paul does not deny their claim head on. It would have been foolish to have done so. But, he points out, just because God has not specifically forbidden something, this does not mean that it is automatically right.

Paul suggests that there are three things to help us determine whether we are in God's will when the action we are thinking of doing is not forbidden by God.

- First of all, we need to ask, 'Is it going to do me any good?' (23). In earlier chapters Paul has applied this principle. In chapter 7, for example, he discusses the question of whether or not it is appropriate to get married. He shows there that a wise decision is not based simply on the general fact that God allows us to do so!

- Secondly, Paul reminds us (as he did in the previous chapter) that there are the needs of others to be considered (23b, 24). Does the thing we are considering build up or destroy the faith of another Christian brother or sister? Paul offers his own life as a model (verse 33). Freedom exercised without considering others is never in the Lord's will!

- Finally, and jumping ahead a little in the passage (11:1), Paul offers a further test which will help us determine God's will. Simply, what would Jesus have done in this situation? Perhaps, for the Corinthians (as for us), this was not easy to find out. They needed to walk closely with Jesus to know how he would have acted. So it is vital to know Jesus well if we are to determine the right course of action when God reveals no clear guidelines to us.

There are occasions when knowing what to do ought to be easy; God has given a clear command. On other occasions it is less simple. Only by reflecting upon the example of Jesus, the needs of others around us and our own well-being can we know what to do. However, there is one other situation that Paul addresses here: knowing what to do when our consciences trouble us but when there seems no reason not to act in a particular way.

What about tender consciences?
Tender consciences (much loved by the Devil) are often troubled by fears and worries that are unnecessary. Paul gives an example here: 'If I go to the butcher's, I don't know whether the meat has been presented as a sacrifice in a pagan temple. What should I do?' His answer is refreshingly clear, 'Don't worry or even think about it. Go ahead and buy the meat!' (25, 26).

Yet this is not his last word! While the purchaser should not worry about it, he ought to be sensitive to those who do (27–29a). The earlier principles, therefore, still apply. While the details of what Paul has to say in these verses are a little unclear because we do not know the precise situation, his main point is clear enough. Once again, what we do is to be determined by the needs and situation of others and not simply ourselves.

Again we struggle to understand Paul in verses 29–30 because we are not fully aware of the background. However, his point would seem to be this: if Paul does something with a clear conscience which is not forbidden by God (or if I do), no-one else has the right to judge his (my) motives: *but* (and it is a big but) we would be wrong to persist in our actions if we were upsetting a friend (28). That would bring us under God's judgment, not for doing whatever it was but for upsetting someone's conscience.

Paul concludes his discussion by re-emphasizing the main principles that should guide all actions (10:31 – 11:1). The Christian is to show respect for God and his will and a desire to please him. This is to be accompanied by the absence of self-seeking and the wish to serve others. Above all, it is to be governed by the question, 'What would

Jesus have done?' This was the standard Paul set for himself; it is one for all other followers of Jesus.

Questions
1. 'I try to please everybody in every way' (33). But Paul often offended people (look at Galatians 5:12). What does he mean?
2. Do you think that verse 20 teaches that all non-Christian religions are basically demonic? Ask those with experience of other religions if you can.
3. What situations in our world today raise difficult moral questions for believers?

Does Paul contradict himself in chapters 8 and 10?

In chapter 8 it seems that Paul is suggesting that it is possible to go to certain events in pagan temples whereas in chapter 10 he forbids this! Presumably Paul was no more likely to contradict himself than we are. How then do we explain this apparent problem?

Two answers seem possible. First of all, in chapter 8 Paul allows the theoretical possibility but in chapter 10 denies it because, as he points out, there are other considerations that rule it out completely.

The alternative explanation is that in chapter 8 Paul is dealing with social gatherings in temples and in chapter 10 has shifted to actual worship in such places. It is not clear which is the more likely.

Passover and the Lord's Supper

In 10:16 Paul refers for the first time to the Lord's Supper, the main theme of the next chapter.

When he uses the phrase 'the cup of blessing' (NIV *thanksgiving*) in 10:16, Jewish readers would immediately have been reminded of the Passover. Paul prepares the way for the next chapter by reminding his readers of the Old Testament and Jewish roots of the Lord's Supper. The 'cup of blessing' was the third of the four special 'cups' drunk at the Passover meal, which every Jewish family celebrated annually to remember the exodus from Egypt. In fact, it was the 'cup of blessing' which Jesus turned into a memorial of his blood (Luke 22:20; 1 Corinthians 11:25).

We can read about the origin of the Passover meal in Exodus 12. If only Israel had remembered that wonderful Passover night, when God

was so close to each of them as they ate the meat of the lamb and prepared to leave Egypt! If they had remembered, they would not have
fallen into the sins Paul describes in 10:7–10. Those sins were the more
horrible because of the beautiful *fellowship with God* which they were
violating – a fellowship symbolized by eating and drinking (10:3–4).

Paul fears the same will be true of the Corinthians. They, too, enjoy a
beautiful fellowship with Christ as they eat and drink with him – but
they could ruin it all by idolatry and self-assertion over the needs of
others. He has already reminded them of this, back in 5:6–8. Referring
to the 'unleavened' or unraised bread eaten at Passover, he tells the
Corinthians to clean up their acts, for 'the Messiah, our Passover Lamb,
has already been sacrificed for the Passover meal, and we are the
Unraised Bread part of the feast. So let's live out our part of the feast,
not as raised bread swollen with yeast and evil, but as flat bread – simple,
genuine, unpretentious' (E. Peterson, *The Message*: NavPress, 1993).

Behind Paul's references to the Passover, of course, lies the Last
Supper of Jesus with his disciples, which was a Passover meal.

WOMEN AND MEN IN WORSHIP
1 Corinthians 11:2–16

1 Corinthians 11:2–6
The role of women in church life

Paul corrects false teaching on the differences between the sexes by offering his own theological answer.

 The argument switches abruptly (in our translations at least) from what Christians should do about idol feasts to the role of women in worship, and Paul dives straight in at the point the Corinthians had raised with him, the question of women's headcovering (2). This is not, perhaps, where we would have started!

We do not know the precise nature of the problem Paul is dealing with here. Does he want the women of Corinth to wear a headcovering (veil) in 'worship' meetings? Or is his concern hair length? Or is he speaking of hairstyle (objecting to women wearing 'loosed hair' instead of hair which was 'piled up' – see Numbers 5:18)? The first and third of these views are the most likely. Paul's only clear reference to hair seems to be an illustration (14, 15), so he is probably dealing here with the wearing of headcoverings.

It is unlikely that this headcovering was the full veil of modern Muslim cultures, which was apparently unknown in those days. Paul probably means the loose end of an outer garment which could be put over the head, or a loosely fitting shawl (from the word used at the end of verse 15).

Paul was a wise pastor! He gives praise where his readers might have been expecting it, before correcting the faults of his people. He had urged the Corinthians to imitate his imitation of Christ (1). So he encourages them with praise about certain unmentioned traditions which they were keeping. Then he proceeds to correct them in several areas, although, in verses 2–16, he does this in a relatively mild way. Perhaps many of the Corinthians already agreed with him.

Who is the head?

It is vital not to become bogged down in the details of a 'squabble' in the church. We need to 'lift our heads' and focus on God! This is what Paul literally does here (3).

Certain Corinthians, as we have already seen, were asserting their individual freedom. In particular, there appear to have been some women who were blurring the distinctions between the sexes (see 5, 6). However, Paul wants them to think of their responsibility in relationships. Since the problem had to do with what women wore on their heads, Paul made them think about another (metaphorical) sense of the word 'head', one which spoke of relationships.

He applies the word 'head' to three relationships: man/Christ; woman/man; Christ/God. Almost certainly, the Corinthians would have understood the Greek word for head to mean 'source', 'origin' or 'fountainhead'. We are probably being influenced by our own culture when we read the word 'head' as 'ruler' or 'boss' (or as referring to 'authority over').

Paul argues that Christ is the source of every Christian man (2 Corinthians 5:17 and compare 1 Corinthians 1:30), or perhaps that Christ is the origin of every man's human life (Colossians 1:15 and see 1 Corinthians 8:6). Again, man was the original source of the woman, a reference to the creation account (8, 12 and Genesis 2). Finally, God was the source of Christ in the incarnation, the Christ who became the source of 'every man'. Thus Paul presses back to the ultimate source of all things, God himself.

Against this background, Paul emphasizes (4) that if the man were to cover his physical head when praying or prophesying it would bring shame to Christ (his 'head') since Christ was the source of his existence.

Does hairstyle matter?

Paul's real concern, however, was with certain women who were not covering their heads in worship (5, 6). It seems that some women were taking part in the church gatherings at Corinth without the customary headcovering (or, perhaps, hairstyle). Perhaps they claimed to be 'spiritual ones' (12:1; 14:37) and to have already entered upon 'resurrection' in baptism (hence the denial of future resurrection, 15:12). They regarded themselves as being 'like the angels' (see Luke 20:35ff.). Another possibility is that perhaps these women carried over into the church the practices of pagan cults. Maybe they were uncovering their hair by removing the loose end of their outer garment from their heads so that they might 'let their hair loose' in the frenzied fashion of cultic prophetesses. Some have suggested that prostitutes in Corinth distinguished themselves by appearing bareheaded in public.

Perhaps they were casting aside tokens of their married state or simply (and more likely) disregarding customary distinctions between the sexes. Paul believes that such women bring shame on the Christian man, disregarding the male/female relationship (3) by making no differentiation between the sexes. This view seems the most likely.

The apostle takes their argument to the extreme to show how wrong they are. He literally says, 'Let her also have her hair cut short.' Such a woman was breaking down the sexual distinctions which prevailed in her culture. 'Let her go the whole way to shame', Paul seems to say, 'by having her hair cut like a man's.'

The precise meaning of this passage will continue to be disputed. Clearly, however, women took part in verbal ministry in the worship meetings of the church and this was accepted by Paul. Some dispute this. However, prophecy was a spiritual gift for the building up of the assembly (see chapter 14) and 'prayer and prophecy' are important parts of such worship meetings. This should guide our practice today (see also on 14:33–35): there must be provision for sisters as well as brothers in Christ to exercise their God-given ministries in church gatherings.

Questions

1. If you are studying in a group you may find that there are different opinions about the role of women in public worship and church leadership. Share these differences honestly and sensitively and discuss them in the light of this passage.
2. How far is God my 'head' and in what sense?
3. What implications does this passage have for the worship practices of our congregation?
4. When is it correct for the church to 'borrow' practices from the surrounding culture?

Head and hair

Bible-believing scholars are still debating whether 'head' (Greek: *kephalē*), when it is used in a non-physical sense in the New Testament (for example in 1 Corinthians 11:3; Ephesians 5:23), means 'authority over' or 'source'. If the view that 'head' means 'authority over' is correct, then it can be argued that the passage teaches that the relative roles of husbands and wives in marriage are applicable in the life and meetings of the church and should be represented by appropriate cultural expressions. The wife, although equal to the husband, is to be subordinate to him on the basis of the order established at creation (8, 9), and this is to be reflected in the worship of the church.

However, it is doubtful whether the Corinthians would have understood the passage in this way. Despite extensive studies which seek to show that 'head' means 'authority over' in ancient Greek literature, the translators of the ancient Greek version of the Old Testament (the Septuagint) apparently didn't think in this way. The Hebrew word for 'head' (*rosh*) often meant 'chief' or 'leader'. When this Hebrew word was used to refer to the physical head, the translators of the Septuagint usually used the word *kephalē*. However, they hardly ever did so when the sense of the Hebrew word (*rosh*) was 'ruler' or 'leader' (which, in any case, is not the same as 'authority over').

Furthermore, in verse 8 Paul appears to refer back to the theological statement of verse 3. He clearly speaks of the woman (at creation) coming 'from' (or 'out of') the man. The idea is clearly that of source of origin.

It could be argued that Paul, rather than teaching subordination in this passage, goes out of his way to deny it (11, 12). God is the ultimate source of all things (12b), before whom men and women stand on an equal footing in the Lord (Christ, 11a).

In many cultures today of course it is no shame for a woman to wear short hair or for a man to have long hair. It is sometimes difficult to tell men and women apart. This would have appalled the early Christians, Greeks and Romans. In blurring the distinction between the sexes, are we denying a fundamental principle or is it merely a cultural fashion?

1 Corinthians 11:7–12

Headcoverings and creation

Men and women are to live as equals without denying the differences that exist between them.

Paul continues his discussion about headcoverings in worship with an argument from the biblical creation account. He does it in a way with which most of us are unfamiliar, so we need to follow him carefully.

Paul does not deny that the woman was created in God's image, or that she brings glory to God (7). Notice that there is not an exact parallel. He speaks of the man as the *image and glory of God*, but of the woman only as *the glory* (not the 'image') *of man*.

Paul refers to the two accounts of the creation of the human race in Genesis 1 and 2. God created mankind as *male and female* in his image (Genesis 1:27). But God created the male person directly (Genesis 2:7). The point seems to be that the existence of the man (created directly) brings honour and praise to God. He is to live in relationship to God so as to bring glory to him. The woman, however, is the glory of the man, since she was created through him (8, 9). The implication is that she is not to pray or prophesy in worship with her head uncovered and therefore bring shame on the man, whose glory she is, by blurring the distinction between the sexes (as it was expressed in that culture).

Paul explains, from the creation account, how the woman is the glory of the man. God did not create the woman directly. She came 'from' (or 'out of') the man (Genesis 2:21ff.). The man is her 'head', that is, her source or origin (3). In this sense, she is his glory.

However, she was also created because of him and not vice versa. Adam needed a helper; none of the animals would do (Genesis 2:18ff.). Therefore, the woman who came 'out of' him 'corresponded' to him (as the Hebrew word indicates) as a partner and equal who, at the same time, complemented him. So, in the Genesis account, we find the man 'glorying' in her – 'At last ... bone of my bone.' In this way *the woman is the glory of man*.

Certain Corinthians needed to realize that the woman, as man's glory, must not bring shame on the man by disregarding customary practices and thus undermining the male/female relationship that still exists in the present age. Paul teaches that the created equality of woman has been restored in Christ (11). However, at the precise point where this is underlined – her sharing with men in the ministries of the church – special care is needed not to blur the male/female distinctions that still exist.

We expect Paul to say here, 'For this reason, a woman ought to have her head covered' (10). That is certainly the thrust of his argument. However, his words here are hard to understand, possibly because he uses terms that were used by these women at Corinth; 'authority' (see 6:12 and 8:9) and 'the angels' (see 'Celestial resurrection' below).

The Greek word for 'authority' is here often translated as 'sign of authority', pointing to the headcovering as the symbol of the husband's authority over his wife. But there is no evidence that the word was ever used in that way. Paul literally writes, 'The woman ought to have authority over her head.' Paul is probably simply referring to the freedom or right of these women to choose what they wear on their heads in worship. No doubt these Corinthian women demanded this choice, linking it with the fact that they were 'like the angels' – they had entered the new age in Christ.

Paul does not dispute the basic truth of all this but suggests that they should freely choose to cover their heads in worship and so maintain the appropriate distinctions between the sexes. This is another example of the principle Paul frequently underlines: you have the choice, but that choice is to be used to benefit others.

So Paul qualifies what he has written (11, 12). The woman may have freedom to choose ('authority over her head'; verse 10), but she is not independent of man. She must bear in mind that in the Christian era man and woman depend on each other completely. And this is not only true in marriage; it is a feature of the life of the new community (the true church).

The man must recognize the same interdependency. Although the woman came 'out of' him and was created 'because' of him (8, 9), each subsequent male person has been dependent on a woman for his birth: 'so also man is born of (or through) the woman'. So Paul argues that each 'came out' of the other. This mutual dependency is 'in the Lord' (11a) and both are ultimately dependent on God.

It is strange that this passage has been used to teach the subordination of the woman to the man in marriage and even the subordination of all women to all men in the church. Paul goes out of his way here to underline the mutual dependency and absolute equality of men and women in Christ. This must be reflected in Christian marriage and church life, even if a case is still made for male leadership. The New Testament does speak of submission, but the emphasis is on submission to one another (Ephesians 5:21ff.).

Questions

1. Do I feel superior/inferior because I am a woman/man? Am I glad to be as I am? How does this passage help me come to terms with my sexuality?
2. How might men and women show their mutual dependence on one another in our church?
3. What are the lessons we can learn from the modern feminist movement and the perils we need to avoid in it?

Celestial resurrection

The underlying error that Paul seems to be dealing with here and elsewhere in 1 Corinthians has been called 'celestial resurrection'.

There were those at Corinth who held to an 'over-realized eschatology'. This means that they regarded as fulfilled ('realized') in the here and now those things which the Bible tells us are to be completely fulfilled in the age to come. Such things are indeed partly fulfilled in the present because the age to come has broken into this age in Christ, but everything has not yet arrived.

These people apparently regarded their baptism as the resurrection to an exalted life here and now. (Note what Paul writes in 4:8.) They claimed to be raised already and so denied future resurrection. Such people regarded themselves as 'like the angels', having the tongues of angels (13:1). Life was essentially an experience of 'spirit'. This led to certain women denying sexual distinctions in practical terms. It may even have led to an implicit denial of their married state since, as 'risen ones', they no longer owed marital allegiance (Luke 20:35ff.: see also 1 Corinthians 7).

There are tendencies towards an over-realized eschatology among certain churches today. This can lead to serious practical difficulties, just as it did at Corinth.

1 Corinthians 11:13–16
Headcoverings and custom

It is important not to do something in the church which would be seen as scandalous by unbelievers, even if believers are free to do so.

We should not regard Paul as making absolute requirements here. Most unusually for him, he appeals to what is 'proper' (13); 'nature' (14); and 'custom' (or 'practice': 16). These vary considerably from age to age, society to society and culture to culture.

Paul asks the Corinthians a question: *Is it proper for a woman to pray to God with her head uncovered?* Addressing people in that culture, he expects the answer, 'No!' He clinches this by asking a further question (14, 15) to which he expects the answer 'Yes'.

The explanation seems to be like this. In Greek-Roman society men normally wore their hair short and women wore their hair long, as can be seen from their paintings, reliefs and sculptures. Paul is not arguing for long or short hair in general. He is simply saying that, in that culture, a woman's long hair (fully seen in the privacy of the home, where she would be free to unbind her hair), needs to be 'covered' (for example, with a shawl) when she prays in worship meetings. On the other hand, men should not have long hair, says Paul. Corinth was into gender-confusion in a big way, and this is what Paul opposes. Men should not make themselves look like women; neither should women behave like men.

He appeals to 'the very nature of things'. Such an appeal, unique in Paul's writings, would have been familiar to some of his readers from current popular philosophy. He is not referring to some 'created order'. He is speaking of the 'natural feeling' that they shared together as part of their contemporary culture.

This is not as forceful an argument as is usual with Paul, so he underlines his advice to them by an appeal to church 'custom' (16). Even then, he does not issue a firm command. To those arguing for no headcoverings, he simply asserts, 'We have no such practice (a better translation than 'no other practice') – nor do the churches of God.'

Paul often appeals to the standards of other churches in this letter (see 4:17; 7:17; and see 14:33). By his words here he gently counters the independent attitude present in the Corinthian church and too often present in churches today. They were to see themselves as part of a larger whole (see on 1:2).

We must be very careful how we apply this passage to church life today. Of course, we are to take account of principles that appear to undergird the passage. However, we cannot be absolutely certain of the details of the local situation and the nature and significance of the practice that Paul was concerned about. Furthermore, the apostle clearly does not regard this matter as a 'big deal'. Compare this low-key approach with his treatment of the abuse of the Lord's Supper, where the very nature of the gospel and the church was at stake.

So we should not make this passage the basis of some sort of canon law (fixed church standards). Indeed, to do so may be to fly in the face of some of the principles in it (such as the equality of men and women in Christ). The most that can be said, given the usually complex nature of the cultures our churches are in, is that there are those modes of dress that are appropriate and those that are not. We certainly should respect conventions! And the very point where the equality of women in Christ is most poignantly to be seen (in their right to participate with men in the ministries and meetings of the church) is where the greatest care is needed not to blur present sexual distinctions.

Questions
1. Is there a danger that I see certain issues in the church as more important than they really are? What are they?
2. Why do Christian congregations so often divide over minor matters?
3. How should Christians dress for worship today? Does it matter? What are we expressing by the way we dress?

THE LORD'S SUPPER
1 Corinthians 11:17–34

1 Corinthians 11:17–22

The Lord's Supper: the problem at Corinth

Paul is concerned that divisions at the Lord's Table denied the very unity of the Lord's Supper.

Paul continues to deal with 'traditions' regarding church worship meetings (2). The problem concerning headcoverings was 'small beer' compared with the abuse of the Lord's Table (see 10:21).

Paul's fundamental concern was the meetings or assemblies of the believers (17, 18, 34 and 14:26), at which there was an 'eating together' (20–22) centred on the bread and cup of the Lord's Supper. This was meant to be the focus of the church's unity (10:17). Instead, it was a forum for 'divisions' (18, 19, 21, 22).

Paul may have learned of these divisions from the Christian slaves of Chloe's household (1:11). However, these are not the same divisions as those he refers to in 1:10, but rather between rich and poor, the 'haves' and the 'have nots'.

These chapters underline the basic idea of 'church' as 'assembly'. To be a member of a church is to meet regularly with other believers, not just to have one's name on a list! Such assemblies are for members to build one another up (see discussion on chapter 14). But, unless we *make every effort to keep the unity of the Spirit* in Christ (Ephesians 4:3), something that was intended for the praise of God's glory and for our benefit can do more harm than good!

Inevitable upsets

The apostle knew Jesus' teaching that his coming would have the effect of dividing households (Matthew 10:34–37), and some people were bound to cause others to stumble (Matthew 18:7). He also believed that Jesus had brought in the 'end-time': the end has come in principle now, although it has not come in the fullest sense of Christ's return.

Although divisions are not good in themselves, they are an inevitable aspect of the end times. They separate true believers from false. In all this, God works out his own purposes. So those who are tested and 'approved' (the word in verse 19 is related to the word 'to examine' in verse 28) emerge clearly. They will escape the world's judgment (32).

The proof that we are truly Christ's, children of the age to come, does not lie simply in our beliefs but in behaviour that reflects the gospel. Only this will pass the 'examination' whenever it comes.

Paul makes the point that although the Corinthians were meeting together in assembly (20), they did not truly eat the Lord's Supper. That meal derived from the Lord's own Last Supper and is eaten by the gathered people of God in his presence and to his honour. In sharp contrast to this, there were those who were eating their own suppers. Verse 21 should be translated: 'For as you eat, each of you goes ahead with his own supper.'

In the early church, the Lord's Supper was eaten as, or in connection with, an ordinary meal (Acts 2:42, 46; 20:7, 11). Such meals were nearly always part of worship in the ancient world (see 10:16–22). Paul does not oppose this 'fellowship meal' (to assume so is to misunderstand what he says in verse 34, as we shall see). His complaint is the treatment of the poor by the rich at the meal.

The 'haves' and the 'have nots'

The meeting-meal was probably hosted by one of the richer Christians. The dining room in such homes accommodated a few guests, usually from the host's own class. At such a communal meal, the majority would have eaten in the entry 'courtyard'. In that culture, the wealthy ate privileged portions not made available to the rest. It is likely that the better-off Christians at Corinth had transferred their regular social practice (natural to them throughout their lives) to the Lord's Supper. The rich were eating their own sumptuous private meals at the Lord's Supper and not sharing their food with the poor. They may well have also begun to eat before others (slaves and others) were able to arrive. Presumably the meal of the latter consisted basically of the bread and wine for the remembrance of Christ. While the 'haves' over-indulged, the 'have nots' went away hungry.

Paul fires off a series of indignant questions (22). In doing so he teaches that the very meaning of the church and the gospel was being undermined! Those who must indulge themselves, he says, should do so in their houses. That, however, is not the purpose of the Lord's Supper (see 23–26) and, in any case, the poor could not do it. The behaviour of these well-off Christians showed a contempt for the church as the community of God's people. They were degrading the Christians who had nothing.

Paul does not at this point call well-off Christians to share with the needy (see 16:1–4). His concern here is the significance of the Lord's Table for the Corinthians' unity in Christ. Let the rich put aside their privileged portions and let there be a common table (even if the fare is simple), without the presence of worldly distinctions! Otherwise the meaning of the Supper itself will be destroyed by the undermining of the very unity it proclaims.

As the people of the new era, the old distinctions which divide human beings must disappear among us. This should certainly be reflected at the Lord's Table where we especially proclaim our unity in Christ.

The distinction between slave and free (or poor and rich) may not be too apparent in the way we conduct the Lord's Supper in our churches. But what about other distinctions, such as that between male and female (see Galatians 3:28)?

Questions

1. What do you think is the point of meeting at the Lord's Table?
2. Plan a communion service for your church which would really express Paul's teaching in this section (and looking ahead to 11:34). With permission, perhaps you could use your service in practice.
3. When our churches meet, are they really showing that the social distinctions that mean so much in the world at large mean nothing in the church?

1 Corinthians 11:23–26

The Lord's Supper: how it was instituted

Paul reminds his readers of some frequently neglected aspects of the Lord's Table.

 The Corinthians had clearly lost touch with the real meaning of the Lord's Supper. Paul reminds them of its institution and its focus on the death-by-crucifixion and (hence) resurrection of Jesus (23, 24). Through these events Jesus had brought into being this last-age fellowship, that is, the church, his body. The Corinthians were not acting consistently with this. By mistreating each other they were abusing him. The Corinthians were keen on traditions but here was one tradition they were not keeping (see verse 2).

Paul did not receive this tradition directly from Jesus (unlike the gospel message itself: see Galatians 1:11, 12). However, it was transmitted by the early Christians under the ultimate supervision of the risen and exalted Lord. We find another form of this tradition recorded in the gospels (for example Mark 14:18–26), but there is no contradiction, and what Paul writes is the same in form as Luke's account despite differences in certain details (see Luke 22:14–23).

The Lord's Supper derives from the last supper that Jesus ate with his disciples, apparently a Passover meal. Unlike the meals of the mystery religions (with their timeless myths), the supper the Corinthians were to celebrate was rooted in history: 'the night [the Lord Jesus] was betrayed'.

The command, *do this in remembrance of me*, could be translated, 'do this for my memorial'. In Old Testament thought, remembrance is a dynamic matter rather than a mere mental activity. The Passover meal itself was a memorial, to be kept for ever in Israel (Exodus 13:9).

125

The Lord's Supper is not merely a commemoration of Christ's death, so that we only think about the cross as we eat the bread and drink the wine. Rather, the actual observation of the Lord's Supper by the true Israel is a memorial of the salvation Jesus Christ has effected. The Corinthians had forgotten this and were undermining the purpose of this salvation, which was to create a new community in which the old distinctions have disappeared. How easy it is for a church to forget or undermine the true significance of the Lord's Supper!

The words that instituted (or established) the Last Supper here recall the ratification of the old covenant (Exodus 24:8) and the prophecy of Jeremiah regarding the replacement of this covenant (Jeremiah 31:31). The wording in Mark's account is different (Mark 14:24) but both Mark's and Paul's accounts make the same point: the wine of the cup signifies Jesus' blood poured out in a death which ratified (or confirmed) the new covenant (or treaty). This is for the church as a group, not just for individuals. To take part in this symbol of the new covenant was to be the covenant community – the new Israel.

Until he comes again

The addition of *whenever you drink it* implies that the Lord's Supper was to be a frequently repeated meal (unlike the annual Passover) in honour of the Lord, but also suggests it would not be too often. While bread was always available, in ordinary households wine was not.

Paul now explains why he had repeated the words of institution since they underlined the fact that the bread and cup of the Lord's meal together signify Christ's death (26). The word order in the original puts the emphasis on Christ's death: 'For (at this meal) ... the Lord's death you proclaim until he comes.'

The use elsewhere of the word translated as *you proclaim* (or declare) suggests that during the meal Jesus' death is declared. This takes place in the two sayings over the bread and cup. These point to his death in the place of others and his confirmation of the new covenant between God and his people by his blood poured out in death.

But the apostle does not view Christ's death as the end event. The Lord's Supper is to be eaten *until he comes* (see Mark 14:25). Christ's death has inaugurated the new era (the end-times), not completed it. Neither had the Corinthians yet 'arrived' (see 4:8). They were to be reminded at this meal that they, together with all God's people, were the people of the age to come.

Questions

1. How does the Lord's Supper/Holy Communion meet our needs? Does it matter that our practices differ from each other's and from the Corinthians'?
2. How often should we celebrate the Lord's Supper? Why?
3. All that Paul records in verses 23–26 speaks of a togetherness in participating in the Lord's meal, over against the self-gratifying individualism present at Corinth. In our case, might it help us to take the bread and wine in conjunction with a fellowship meal sometimes? If we already do, is it helpful? Why?

My body which is for you

In Jewish homes the meal began with the family head breaking and distributing the bread with an appropriate prayer of blessing. At the Passover meal this took place during the meal (Mark 14:18; Luke 22:17–19), following the declaration of the reasons for this meal, which were rooted in the history of salvation (see Exodus 13:8). Jesus reinterpreted the meaning of this bread (and later the wine) in terms of his own death.

The history of the church has been riddled with controversy over the words *This is my body, which is for you*. This is because Greek ways of thinking gradually came into the church. Given the Jewish background of the Last Supper, Jesus could only have meant something like 'This (bread) signifies my body'.

The full expression, as recorded by Luke and Paul, interprets Jesus' death in the light of Isaiah 53 as on behalf of others; even in the place of those who eat at the Table. In Isaiah 53:12 we read of the Suffering Servant that *he bore the sin of many*.

1 Corinthians 11:27–34

The Lord's Supper: the remedy to the problem

Where the church's practice at the Lord's Table is not what God wishes, steps need to be taken to put the matter right!

Paul applies what he has been saying to correct the specific error of the well-off going ahead with their own private meals to the neglect of the poor. He warns them of the consequences of their failure to understand the true nature of the Supper.

Unworthy to take the Lord's Supper?

Paul picks up the language of verses 23–26 concerning eating and drinking and body and blood (27). His concern is with those who take part in the Lord's Supper *in an unworthy manner*. Unfortunately, the KJV translated this as 'unworthily', and this, together with a narrow view of the 'sacrament', has led many Christians to be fearful and negative about the Lord's Table. They fear to come to communion because of 'sin' in their lives which they think might disqualify them in God's eyes.

The kind of 'unworthiness' Paul means, however, is described in verses 17–22. It is a question of divisions; of abuse of other believers at the Lord's Table; of missing the point of the meal as a proclamation of salvation through Christ's death, a salvation which constituted Christ's new community where there is 'the unity of the Spirit'. Nobody should be excluded because of sinful weakness or failure to be in a suitably spiritual frame of mind. Should we stay away from the fountain because we are thirsty?

This being said, to profane the Lord's meal by such abuse as Paul describes here is extremely serious. It is (literally) to 'be guilty of the body and blood of the Lord'. It is to be liable for that very death that should be proclaimed as salvation at the Lord's Table. So the Corinthians were to examine themselves before eating (28).

This, again, is not meant to lead to unhealthy self-examination. Rather, Paul calls for a right attitude and, especially, right behaviour to those gathered at the Table (29). God will judge a wrong attitude so it is best to judge ourselves first (30–32). In any case coming casually to the Lord's Table is wrong. It is a serious matter.

Are you staying away from the Lord's Supper because of personal sin and failure? You have no warrant to do so; it is a greater sin to stay away. On the other hand, is there too casual an approach to 'communion' in our churches? To participate properly is to be prepared to submit to the gospel that is proclaimed, with all its implications.

'Discerning the body'

The phrase *without recognising* (or discerning) *the body* (29) probably means the church as the body of Christ. Although the term 'body' has come from the references to Christ's physical body given in death, represented by the bread (23, 24 and 27), in the background are Paul's words in 10:17. There, he declared that their all sharing the 'one loaf' showed the Corinthians that they themselves were therefore 'one body'. Paul is concerned that the church members have not seen themselves as a united body ('discern the body') because they are divided into the 'haves' and 'have nots'.

The Lord's Supper is not just a meal. With one loaf and a common cup we proclaim that through the death of Christ we are one body in Christ. We must not allow social distinctions at this Table. We are the one body of Christ in which we are all gifts to each other.

The apostle then makes a prophetic statement (30). Many were ill among the Corinthian Christians and a number of deaths had occurred. The victims were not necessarily the people who had sinned against others. But Paul sees that, in this case, the whole community has experienced judgment through the actions of some at the Lord's Supper.

This was a prophetic insight into the situation of the Corinthians, not to be rashly applied in considering the situation of another church (for example, today!). Paul is not saying that sickness among Christians is normally to be viewed as present judgment. However, it is interesting to compare James 5:14–16, where the word translated as 'sick' is the same as that translated as 'weak' in 1 Corinthians 11:30. Calling the elders together perhaps suggests that sin against the fellowship had occurred, clearly a serious matter!

Getting it right

If the Corinthians had been 'discerning the body' they would not have been experiencing judgment. However, even God's judgment towards believers is full of mercy (31, 32). Here 'judgment' does not refer to eternal salvation but a divine discipline in which a loving God corrects his children precisely so that they will not be condemned with the world at the final judgment.

By way of direct application, Paul first tells the Corinthians that when they come together to eat they should wait for each other (33, 34). This applied particularly to the well-off Christians who were going ahead and eating their delicacies regardless of the poor Christians (21, 22). The word translated 'wait for' may in fact have the sense 'receive' or 'welcome'.

Secondly, if the wealthy wanted to eat the kind of sumptuous meals they normally ate together they should do this in private at home, apart from the Lord's meal (to the humiliation of the 'have nots'). In the community, the well-off should eat what the others do rather than shaming them. Of course, the 'hidden agenda' is that the well-off should share what they have with the less well-off (see Romans 12:13). But his first concern is that the gospel and the unity proclaimed at this meal remain intact.

The main concern of this passage has to do with fellowship and relationships in the body of Christ. Certainly, our gathering at the Lord's Supper is to be rooted in Jesus' crucifixion and resurrection. However, we must remember the purpose of the salvation that these achieved and ensure that the Lord's Supper is the focus of the oneness of the new community. We must give proper attention to our relationships with each other.

The climax of the passage is clear enough. As we gather at the Lord's Table we are to receive and welcome one another, as beneficiaries of Christ's death, participating afresh in the benefit of that death precisely as we do so.

Questions

1. Are there any occasions when it would be right *not* to take the bread and wine at communion?
2. What have you found most helpful in sharing the Lord's Supper and in preparing for it?
3. What distinctions lead *us* to fail to discern the body at the Lord's Supper (see 1 Corinthians 12:13; Galatians 3:28)?
4. How far are we living as a new and alternative community in the eyes of the outside world?

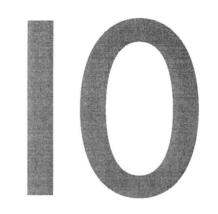

SPIRITUAL
GIFTS

1 Corinthians 12:1–30

1 Corinthians 12:1–3
Testing the spirits

This section in his letter deals with spiritual gifts. Paul begins with a warning: not everything that seems spiritual is genuine.

In chapters 12–14 Paul continues to focus on the worship meetings of the Corinthian church (compare 11:17 and 14:23), dealing, in particular, with the use of 'speaking in tongues' in public.

In chapter 12 Paul emphasizes the reality and the need for a variety of spiritual gifts. The theme of chapter 13 is the centrality of love in the Christian life; without it all spiritual gifts are worthless. The specific application of spiritual gifts in the church is dealt with in chapter 14, in particular the misuse of the gift of tongues. Paul points out that spiritual gifts are for the building up of the church. He ends this section with further instructions for orderly worship within the Corinthian church.

The 'spiritually gifted ones'

Paul begins his discussion (1), apparently in response to a point raised in the Corinthians' letter (compare 7:1), by picking up a term evidently favoured by the Corinthians: *pneumatikoi*. This may be translated as 'spiritual gifts' (14:1) or 'spiritually gifted ones' (14:37). The word probably includes both meanings. Paul's preferred term for spiritual gifts is *charismata* (4, 9, 31). Both terms are valid, the one emphasizing the Spirit (*pneuma*), the other the gift or concrete expression of grace (*charis*).

In the background is the whole debate between Paul and the Corinthians about true spirituality. Some people at Corinth felt that they were truly 'spiritual', disregarding bodily existence and believing that they were already like the angels. They considered that their spirituality was shown by their speaking in angelic dialects in the Spirit (13:1). Paul viewed 'life in the Spirit', however, as involving:

- power through present weakness (2:1–5; 2 Corinthians 12:9ff.)

- responsible relationships in Christ's body (14:2) and

- an anticipation of a yet more glorious future through bodily resurrection (chapter 15).

The apostle reminds the Corinthians of their pagan past, and of their former devotion to idols which could neither hear nor speak. He has previously linked such idols with demons (10:20, 21) who could speak through idol worshippers. The unusual combination of verbs which Paul uses in verse 2 (speaking of them being literally 'carried away' and 'led about'), seems to be referring to the ecstatic experiences they had in their pagan cults involving inspired speech. The worshippers were 'possessed'; under the control of a spirit from outside themselves.

The key point is that not all 'inspired' speech is the activity of the Holy Spirit (3). The Corinthians had become infatuated with inspired speech (in the form of 'tongues') for its own sake.

Perhaps those who engaged in 'inspired' speech under the control of spirits said such blasphemous things as *Jesus be* (or is) *cursed*. Paul's point is that no inspired speech, for example tongues, is evidence in itself of the Holy Spirit's activity. This requires clear communication in words that exalt Christ.

True spirituality exalts Jesus as Lord

Now to us it may sound an easy matter to say *Jesus is Lord* (the earliest Christian confession, Romans 10:9). But for the first Christians this was impossible *except by the Holy Spirit*. To say such words at that time was to take a radical step, for they implied absolute allegiance to Jesus as one's God, pointing to the resurrection and exaltation over all (lordship) of the Crucified One. Those words radically distinguished true believers from Jews, for whom such words would have been blasphemy, and from pagans, whose cult-deities were called 'lords' (see 8:5).

Paul is not giving a test to distinguish between true and false inspired speech, but to establish who has the Holy Spirit in his or her life. Christ-exalting confession is the 'bottom line' as a proof of the powerful presence of the Holy Spirit. Inspired speech, however impressive, is not itself evidence of being under the control of the Holy Spirit. Pagans can engage in it (see also Matthew 7:22, 23).

There has been renewed emphasis recently on the Holy Spirit and Spirit-given ministries. We should welcome this as a return to a biblical perspective. However, there is a danger: power and gifts are not the infallible evidence of the Holy Spirit's activity. The real test is the exaltation of Jesus as Lord (John 16:13). Fascination with spiritual activity as an end in itself is in fact paganism, whatever other name we give it! It is like a 'lover' who is more interested in sex than in the one loved. Who, then, is truly 'spiritual'? Paul's answer is given in terms of one's attitude to Christ.

Questions
1. Am I more interested in spiritual gifts than in living for Jesus? Where should my emphasis be?
2. What are the marks of true spirituality? Make a list.
3. How will the unbelieving world be won for Christ?

1 Corinthians 12:4–7
Different gifts, one giver

Paul shows that every true Christian has been gifted by the Spirit for the benefit of other believers.

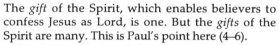

The *gift* of the Spirit, which enables believers to confess Jesus as Lord, is one. But the *gifts* of the Spirit are many. This is Paul's point here (4–6).

For the remainder of this chapter Paul emphasizes the diversity that is basic to the unity of the church, as shown by the wide variety of ways in which the one Spirit chooses to work within the church. But the Corinthians were emphasizing one particular spiritual gift (see 14:1–25). Notice that Paul uses the word translated as 'different kinds of' three times, pointing to differences or varieties (see also verse 11). All this is rooted in the character of God himself; for he is characterized by diversity in unity.

The charismata

In this passage Paul makes three points about the *charismata*.

1. Fundamental to all Christians

   Paul here uses the word *charismata* (gifts) for the first time in these chapters. He gave this word new prominence, if he did not in fact invent it. It occurs sixteen times in his letters; the only other biblical occurrence is in 1 Peter 4:10–11. He uses the word elsewhere to speak of the gift of salvation and eternal life and indeed to point to Christ himself (Romans 5:15, 16; 6:23). These are the fundamental gifts of God and they undergird whatever other 'presents' the Lord may give to believers.

The emphasis then is on God's grace in giving his own presence to all believers, *not* on our reception of specific gifts. So the term 'charismatic movement' to describe those who value the exercise of certain 'gifts' is misleading if it excludes other Christians. For all Christians are truly charismatic in the fullest sense of that term. All true Christians have received God's gift of grace or *charisma* and his Holy Spirit (see Romans 9:9). We all share the full gift of salvation. Let us not set up false distinctions between believers.

2. All gifts and talents are for serving God

Paul here applies the word *charismata* to *service* and *working*. In these verses we meet all three persons of the Trinity. Paul speaks of the *same Spirit* (the Holy Spirit), *the same Lord* (the Son of God or exalted Christ) and *the same God* (the Father). We must not read into these verses (4–6) that the Spirit dispenses the gifts, the Son is in charge of service and the Father is concerned with works. No, there is one God who gives himself to us in a great variety of gifts and ministries.

So the term *charismata* includes everyday acts of service and working as well as the more miraculous gifts. It points to the effective power of God in the broadest sense in all church members. It suggests that we must not distinguish sharply between (so-called) 'charismatic' gifts and 'natural' abilities. All are described as 'manifestations' of the Spirit (7), demonstrations, for all to see, of what God is doing in us all.

3. Gifts cannot be pigeon-holed!

The key word in this sections is *variety*. These verses are probably not meant to be technical instruction about certain precisely definable 'charismatic gifts', but an illustration of how varied the work of God's Spirit is. He is 'the same spirit' (8, 11), but he 'works' and 'gives' many different gifts and ministries. So we should not be jealous of the gifts of others, if they are different from ours.

Nor should we feel left out. Paul emphasizes that God works 'in all people' (6 – not just 'men' as the NIV translates it), 'to each one' (7), 'to each person' (11). God may not give us one of the gifts listed in 8–10, because these are just examples. But he certainly gives a gift or ministry to every Christian.

The showing of the Spirit is *for the common good*. The Corinthians were turning their assemblies into meetings for private religious experiences. Paul's great concern is that Christians realize that the 'gifts' are not given for personal reasons, although the individual believer does benefit (see 14:4), but for the building up of the church community as a whole.

Questions

1. Too often, interest in the Spirit's activity and spiritual gifts has been selfishly motivated. Is our concern for personal satisfaction or glory or for the common good?
2. Our word 'working' comes from a Greek word which suggests 'energy'. Make a list of the different sorts of divine energy at work in people.
3. Are spiritual gifts, services and energies rightly used in your church? How could things be better?

1 Corinthians 12:8–11
Just some of the gifts

Paul describes the marvellously varied ways that the one God gives gifts to all his children.

Paul lists some of the 'manifestations' of the Spirit here (8–10). There are other lists of spiritual gifts both in this chapter and in Paul's other writings (28; Romans 12:6–8; Ephesians 4:11. See also 1 Peter 4:11). They are compiled to illustrate the writer's point in each specific situation, and therefore the lists differ, but there is overlap between them too.

Wisdom and knowledge

Paul lists a range of gifts, mainly of the more extraordinary ('supernatural') kind (although note that such 'ordinary' gifts of helping and administration (28) are regarded as 'charismatic' (31)). In view of the Corinthians' emphasis on the gift of 'tongues' (see chapter 14) he wants to make it clear that it is not the only gift; the others are at least equally important.

Nobody can be certain of the precise nature and meaning of several of these gifts. Perhaps in the long run it doesn't matter, but we will try to understand what we can of the rich diversity of gifts which Paul is stressing to the Corinthians.

It is probably virtually impossible to distinguish between 'the word of knowledge' and 'the word of wisdom', since Paul was probably referring to the 'wisdom' and 'knowledge' that the Corinthians emphasized so much. Most modern definitions ignore this. Indeed, the list clearly reflects the Corinthian situation, with the messages of 'wisdom' and 'knowledge' placed at the beginning (*cf.* 1:5–7) and 'tongues' (with interpretation) at the end.

'Wisdom' and 'knowledge' were clearly key words at Corinth, with its Greek culture. 'Wisdom' was the theme of chapters 1 and 2 and 'knowledge' was referred to in chapter 8. There real wisdom was set over against 'the wisdom of this world and age' (1:20; 2:6), so 'the message of wisdom' surely means a true perception of the mind of Christ, (2:16), an insight into the gospel (centring on Christ crucified) and its implications.

In the context of this letter, 'the word of knowledge' can hardly be the gift of discerning what illness or problem a member of the congregation needs to be healed from. It is more likely that it means a Christ-centred understanding of the Old Testament with the ability to explain both this and Christian traditions.

Faith, healings and miraculous powers

'The same Spirit' (9, *cf.* 4ff.) gives 'faith'. All believers possess saving faith, but Paul appears to be describing here a special gift for a specific circumstance or special service. The example is sometimes given of George Müller who set up an orphanage in Bristol in the last century and relied on God 'by faith' to provide food, clothing and other necessities. Not everyone is expected to live like this but Müller was given the ability to trust God for these things.

Here, therefore, is a supernatural faith that can 'move mountains' (13:2), which is virtually inseparable from 'gifts of healings' and 'miraculous powers'. Note that these two gifts are mentioned in the plural. This probably suggests that each occurrence of one person physically healing another is a specific gift; that a Christian may be granted the *charisma* to heal a particular individual of his or her specific disease on a certain occasion; that every healing, as a special gift, involves new dependence on the divine Giver. If this is so, there is no basis for expecting healing after every prayer or for the founding of a 'healing ministry'. Such gifts of healings are included in 'miraculous powers' (see Acts 2:22, 43), but this manifestation presumably also covers all other kinds of supernatural activity, such as exorcisms. (Note the plural again, pointing to the same sort of diversity as the previous gift.)

Prophecy

A further supernatural activity is added: 'prophecy' (10: see 'Prophecy and preaching', p. 165). It is clear from chapter 14 that this prophecy involves Spirit-inspired speech that was basically spontaneous, understandable and orally delivered in the assembly for the purpose of encouraging and building up the gathered believers.

Discerning of spirits

'Distinguishing between spirits' (or, more literally, 'discernings of spirits', 10) seems to relate especially to 'prophecy' (as 'interpretation' does to 'tongues'). Prophecy should be assessed by 'the others' (see 14:29). It is possible that this is the ability to discern what is truly of the Spirit of God and what comes from other, perhaps demonic, spirits. It needs profound doctrinal awareness (1 John 4:1ff.). However, what is more to the point is Paul's own use of the word 'spirit(s)' in 14:14 and 32, where the Spirit who speaks through the prophets is understood to be speaking through the spirits of the prophets. The apostle mainly has in mind the gift of discerning, or properly judging, prophecies, as described in 14:29. So here, it does not seem to be a question of separating those inspired by the Holy Spirit and those under demonic control, but of underlining the actual utterances of the prophets so that others in the community who have the Spirit can discern what is truly of the Spirit.

Tongues

Speaking in different kinds of tongues (known as *glossolalia*: 10), as chapter 14 makes clear, refers to Spirit-inspired utterances, which neither the speaker nor the hearers can understand (see 'Speaking in tongues', p. 141).

The interpretation of tongues

This gift involves putting into known words, for the benefit of the community, what the tongues-speaker has said, the effect then being like prophecy (14:5). This is seen as a Spirit-inspired utterance granted either to the tongues-speaker or to another (14:5, 13, 27–28).

Implications

In verse 11 Paul sums up what he has said so far. Note that the Spirit is said to 'give' these gifts. To speak of 'the gifts *of* the Spirit' can be misleading since his special task is to distribute those gifts of which God in Christ is the source (28; Romans 12:3; Ephesians 4:7ff.). The Spirit's varied and active work here is underlined in the statement that *he gives them* (individually) *to each one*, and the Spirit does this *just as he determines* (or pleases). How tremendous! The gifts, in all the richness of their diversity, are, in the last analysis, expressions of the Spirit's own sovereign action in the lives of individual believers and of the community as a whole. All this goes against a preoccupation with gaining this or that specific gift for oneself. It does not go against seeking the best gifts (31), but it leads us ultimately to trust in the wisdom of the Holy Spirit to share them out appropriately.

We ought to look for and delight in a gracious diversity of gifts and ministries in each church. Rather than regarding one particular gift as a sign of spirituality, we ought to see the Holy Spirit in the whole range. One Christian leader has said, 'It is reasonable to assume ... that any contribution by any member of the community of a constructive nature would be recognized by Paul as a gift.' At the same time, we cannot ignore the matter-of-fact way in which Paul lists a whole range of extraordinary phenomena as distributed among church members. Do some of us expect a less supernatural dimension to the life of the church today and settle for what is only ordinary? Have we then lost touch with the Spirit of God?

Questions
1. What gifts has God given to me and how do I use them?
2. Is our church's life ordinary? What evidences of God's power are there among us?
3. Would Paul encourage Christian doctors and nurses to think that they were exercising spiritual gifts through medical treatment? Or are healing gifts independent of medicine?

Speaking in tongues

Different kinds of tongues appears at the end of the list of spiritual gifts in 1 Corinthians 12:7–11 and again in verses 28–31. It was not the most important gift, but then, as now, it aroused great controversy because it was spectacular and apparently miraculous. 'Tongues' means speaking aloud in a language unfamiliar to the speaker. Occasionally it is a recognized foreign language, but usually a mixture of sounds which needs an interpreter to make it understandable.

Three comments may help to make things clearer:

1. At Pentecost (Acts 2:1–13) the disciples openly praised God and were heard and understood by visitors to Jerusalem who heard their own languages and dialects. This is the only instance of its kind in the Bible and marked the coming of the Holy Spirit to the church. There was obviously no need for interpretation by a third party.

2. In Corinth the believers used the gift of tongues differently. Many of them appeared to believe that they were speaking the language of angels (see 13:1), a sign that they had 'arrived' spiritually. Their words, however, could not be understood without a third party who

had the gift of interpretation (12:10). This seems to have been a form of prophecy – a means whereby God imparted messages to his people. But some Corinthians were so excited about the exercise of their gift that they were overusing it in their services without interpretation, causing offence to visitors and confusing fellow Christians. Paul makes his views about this clear in 14:1–25.

3. Today the gift of tongues is seen by some, especially in the Pentecostal churches, as important evidence of the reception and presence of the Holy Spirit. It is not seen as the language of angels but mostly as a form of freedom of utterance where words are not enough. It is frequently used in private devotions and also in prayer for individuals for healing and spiritual help.

Opinions are sharply divided about the nature and practice of tongues-speaking today. Paul welcomed the gift (14:18) but urged caution, sensitivity and love for others in its use. Without belittling tongues as a gift from God, it is only fair to add that the phenomenon, or something very like it, happens outside Christian circles too.

1 Corinthians 12:12–20
One body: many limbs

God wants his people to be a body and has gifted them so that they can function that way.

 In verses 1–11 Paul has described the many different gifts. Now he shows how each gift is like a part of the body, and emphasizes the need for unity. The statement *So it is with Christ* (12) not only points to *the body of Christ* (27), but also serves to suggest the closeness of the relationship between Christ and his people (see Acts 9:4).

The imagery of 'the body' was common in the ancient world, although Paul uses it in a special way (see 10:17 and 11:29). In verse 12 Paul stresses both sides of the picture – first, the oneness of the body, and secondly, its diversity. His point is that true unity is the opposite of the sameness the Corinthians were fond of (in their emphasis on tongues) and which is too often apparent (in varying ways) in our churches today.

Unity
Verse 13 continues the theme of verse 12; the body is one. What makes the Corinthians one, Paul tells them, is their common experience of the Spirit; the reality of 'one Spirit' (who is behind the diversity described in verses 4–11) is shared by 'all'. To show that the many have become one, Paul refers to basic distinctions that separated people in his world: race and religion ('Jews or Greeks') and social status ('slave or free'). The shared life of the Spirit has done away with the old distinctions in the one body of Christ. If only we would live as if we knew that this was true!

The various details of verse 13 have wrongly been used to support

143

certain theories about baptism and post-conversion blessings. However, such confusion is unnecessary since the basic point is clear. Paul, against his Jewish background, uses two parallel statements which make the same point in two ways; *we were all baptised by one Spirit* and *we were all given the one Spirit to drink.* They would appear to have been understood in the following way.

The word 'baptism' points to the beginning of the Christian life. We should probably translate *by one Spirit* as 'in one Spirit'. The point is not that the Spirit performs the baptism but that the believer is immersed in the Spirit just as a baptized person is immersed in water (see Matthew 3:11 and Acts 1:5). So believers then have been both immersed in the Spirit and caused to drink to their fill of the Spirit (*cf.* John 7:37–39). Through this experience they have been incorporated into the reality of the one body (outwardly undertaken by water baptism).

To the question, 'When are believers baptized with the Holy Spirit?' the answer given in this verse is: at the time of their incorporation into the one body (at conversion). We share then in the gift of the Spirit with whom Christ baptized the church at Pentecost (Acts 1:5; 2:1–4). However, the words used to describe the Spirit's work do appear to suggest something deeper than we usually expect (see Romans 5:5).

Diversity

The next point, made with urgency, is that even though they are one body, with a shared experience of the Spirit, the body does not consist of one member but many (14). Precisely because they are one body there is a need for diversity. Paul goes on to develop the picture of one body and many parts.

Note that Paul sees the common activity of the Holy Spirit in believers' lives as the basis of true unity. How tragic that this very activity has often been the focus of disunity among Christians! On the other hand, it is not human programmes that will achieve the unity which all true Christians must desire (although they must *make every effort*, Ephesians 4:3), but a powerful work of God's Spirit.

Paul explains this idea of the church as the body of Christ more fully (15, 16). He has the church at Corinth in view (27), so we must be careful not to apply every specific detail but rather pick up the main lessons.

Paul relates certain parts of the body (foot and hand, ear and eye) to real people. His point is that they must not think of themselves as inferior if they appear to have only a small part to play in church life. Everyone is important. Perhaps those who did not speak in tongues were made to feel they did not belong. Paul rejects this (17); all gifts are equally necessary.

Responding to his own questions (18), Paul continues with the imagery of the physical body (as he does until verse 27). How encouraging to know that as we each exercise our ministry in the church to benefit our brothers and sisters, the functions we fulfil are by God's arrangement and in accordance with his will! Let no-one deprive us of our rightful contentment and joy. The body's diversity is God's design.

The Corinthians had unbounded enthusiasm for tongues (uninterpreted tongues being prominent in their assemblies; see 14:24). However, a body consisting of a single organ (whether, in the case of the church, that be, for example, tongues, or even teaching) would be no body at all (19). A self-existing giant eyeball or hand would be a monstrosity! Diversity is essential! The reality of the situation, as verses 12–14 have already indicated, is that there are many parts and one body.

Questions

1. Am I envious of other people's gifts and talents? Write a letter to yourself from Paul about this.
2. Is our church a giant eyeball? How can the variety of gifts be better expressed?
3. How should we understand the remarkable spiritual experiences which many Christians have today?

1 Corinthians 12:21–30
A body needs to look after itself!

Paul reminds the Corinthians that members of the body should live for one another.

Here Paul paints a picture of the different parts of the body talking to one another, each claiming to be superior to the others. The Corinthian Christians who regarded tongues as the mark of spirituality probably looked down on other Christians not possessing that mark (a danger sometimes present today). Paul, however, is more concerned with a general principle, and so we must remember that those who oppose tongues-speaking 'charismatics' today can be equally guilty of spiritual élitism (after all, they don't need tongues; they have a mature grasp of doctrine!).

There were, of course, other divisions in the Corinthian church. Paul has just been writing (11:17–34) about the division between the 'haves' and the 'have nots' which expressed itself at the Lord's Table. Indeed, this may not be far from Paul's mind here.

Nothing can be more destructive of the unity of a church, or more hurtful to individual Christians, than for one Christian to claim superiority over another Christian and his or her gifting. So Paul says that those parts of the body that seem to be weaker are like internal organs, working away out of sight but essential nevertheless (22). And there are other organs (the 'less honourable' and 'unpresentable' are probably the sexual organs) which we treat with special honour by covering them (23).

We will run into difficulties if we try to find people and gifts in our church situation to fit precisely the terms of the picture! The key lesson is that all church members are necessary to the proper functioning of the body. We must all honour gifts which might easily be overlooked. We may often find that they are more indispensable than the more obvious 'up-front' gifts. Instead of division in the church, there should be equal concern for each other (24b, 25). Unity is to be reflected in care for each other.

The whole body shares the good and bad experiences of its members (26). We all know that if we hit our thumb with a hammer the thumb will not suffer in isolation! We will be conscious of the pain in our whole body and unable to give attention to other matters until it is dealt with. Within the church we all need each other and our lives are inextricably bound up together in Christ. What a glorious fellowship!

The principle applied

The word 'you' is emphasized in verse 27. Paul tells the Corinthians that they – yes, with all their problems – were not just a part of the whole church. They were the church – the expression of the one church, in this case in Corinth. They represent Christ; they make up his one body. The stress is again on the many who give the body its necessary diversity.

So Paul makes a second list to illustrate the diversity of gifts God has given to the church (28). But here he focuses upon people rather than gifts.

The Corinthian church was founded by Paul, the apostle (9:1, 2), and the wider ministry of apostles had (and has) a bearing on all local churches. While, potentially, all believers might prophesy (see 14:1), those who did so regularly were known as 'prophets'. In the same way, the gift of teaching is referred to in 14:6 and 26, but those who exercised it regularly were known as 'teachers' (see Acts 13:1). Such a ministry may be linked with 'the word of wisdom' and 'the word of knowledge' (see verse 8). It has been suggested that 'teachers' passed on and interpreted the apostolic traditions (together, perhaps, with giving Christ-centred exposition of the Old Testament).

The listing of apostles, prophets and teachers as 'first', 'second' and 'third' (28) probably simply points to the order in which each ministry appeared in the founding and building up of local assemblies, not to their importance.

The other gifts in the list were referred to in the discussion on verses 8–10, except for *those able to help others* and *those with gifts of administration*, or (perhaps better) 'gifts of support' and 'gifts of direction'. The first word points to all kinds of assistance, and the second perhaps to the giving of wise counsel in order to guide the community.

It is interesting that Paul places such gifts alongside *gifts of healing* and *kinds of tongues* (see 31). This is hardly in line with the emphasis of certain Christians today, or the Corinthians then! We need to submit our differences and presuppositions to Scripture.

The gift of tongues is listed last probably because of its abuse in the Corinthian assemblies.

Paul's second 'list of gifts' leads to a long list of questions (29, 30). He expects a firm negative after each one: *Are all apostles?* 'No!' ... *Do all speak in tongues?* 'No!' *Do all interpret?* 'No!' Paul, in effect, tells the Corinthians to apply the principle here to their emphasis on tongues (even though, as chapter 14 makes clear, he does not disparage the gift of tongues itself, or its interpreted use in Christian assemblies).

Of course, there is nothing in principle to prevent any Christian receiving any of the gifts. But, in God's arrangement, and in practice, all Christians do not function in the same way. What Paul's questions amount to are a plea for diversity.

With the words *But eagerly desire the greater gifts* (31), Paul begins the argument which he develops in chapter 14, where he encourages the exercise of gifts of intelligible speech in the worship meetings. These are 'greater' than tongues because they can directly build up whereas tongues without interpretation cannot.

However, he interrupts this argument with the words, *and now* (or yet) *I will show you the most excellent way* or 'a way that is beyond comparison'. Instead of their present way of exalting private religious experience, destructive to the church as a community, they were called to a way that put the good of others first. The proper framework in which the 'greater gifts' were to function was love. So, before Paul resumes his very practical argument, we are led into the riches of chapter 13 and the so-called 'hymn to love'.

Questions
1. What gifts do I think are most important? Would Paul and God agree with me?
2. What gifts has God given to our congregation? How might we make better use of them?
3. What motive should we all have in the exercise of spiritual gifts? Can it be said to be true in our fellowship?

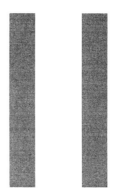

THE MORE EXCELLENT WAY
1 Corinthians 13:1–13

1 Corinthians 13:1–3
Love's necessity

The greatest spiritual gifts and the most zealous religious actions are of no value to us unless our lives are motivated by love.

 This beautiful chapter, often referred to as a 'hymn to love', contains riches enough on its own. But it is part of Paul's argument and gives impetus to what he goes on to write in chapter 14. When it is understood in this way its riches become even more obvious to us. Paul is discussing the Corinthians' preoccupation with the gift of tongues and their abuse of it in their assemblies by having no interpretation (14:23). Also in view is Paul's whole debate with the Corinthians about spirituality and their emphasis on wisdom (chapter 1), knowledge (chapter 8), tongues (chapter 14) and religious activity generally, to the neglect of love, which should be the foundation of all Christian living.

In this chapter, Paul compares love with spiritual gifts. In the latter part he contrasts the permanence (and supremacy) of love with the temporary (and partial) nature of spiritual gifts, but he does not deny the value of the gifts. Love is not an alternative to spiritual gifts nor is it the ultimate spiritual gift. In fact, love is not a gift at all.

In speaking of love, Paul is concerned with a whole way of life, 'the way that is beyond comparison' (12:31b). His main concern is not even that the use of gifts be motivated by love, although that is implied. Rather, unless their use is accompanied by a whole life lived after love's pattern, there is no genuinely Christian substance to them; they are worse than useless. This means that the Corinthian Christians must no longer have a selfish concern for personal religious experience and ability but must seek and exercise expressions of the Spirit with a view to building up their brothers and sisters in community (14:1).

Christian love must be understood in terms of God's love in Christ (Romans 5:6–8). Thus we are to see Christ himself portrayed in verses 4–7. And the love Paul speaks of is neither sentimental nor vague: love is active; it is behaviour; it is to act towards others as God in Christ acts towards us.

Paul brings the matter home (1) by speaking in the first person ('I') and by giving the example of the gift of tongues, since this was the problem at Corinth. He then goes on (1–3) to list a range of gifts (drawn from 12:8–10) and religious activities, showing that love alone is indispensable.

Love and tongues

The expression, *the tongues ... of angels*, may point to the way the Corinthians viewed speaking in tongues; they perhaps believed it was the language of heaven. Angels were believed to have their own heavenly language that could be spoken by human beings by means of the Spirit. Some at Corinth apparently felt they had arrived at the ultimate spiritual condition already; they were like the angels in heaven, so they spoke in 'the tongues of angels'.

Paul's point is this: no matter how exalted the gift of tongues a person possesses, without love he or she is only a resounding gong (an empty, hollow sound) or a clanging cymbal (12:2; associated with the ecstatic worship of pagan cults in those days) and no better than a pagan.

Love and other gifts

Paul goes on to list other *charismata* which are representative of the whole range of spiritual gifts (2): prophecy (see chapter 14), knowledge (so important to the Corinthians, and, in its valid form, basic to the teaching ministry) and faith (special faith for mighty works). By emphasizing the word 'all' Paul tells the Corinthians that if someone could embrace the whole range of *charismata* and possess each one of them in full measure, but should fail to be truly loving, that person would be 'nothing' – that is, nothing in the sight of God.

Even great deeds of personal sacrifice (3) are of no spiritual profit to the one who performs them, if they do not flow from a whole lifestyle characterized by the love described in 4–7.

Selling all one's property to feed the poor (3a) recalls the words of Jesus in Matthew 19:21. In verse 3b Paul could be referring to the fiery ordeal of personal martyrdom. If, on the other hand, Paul speaks of surrendering his body 'that I may boast', then the word 'boast' must be meant positively (see 1:29–31; 9:15; 2 Corinthians 1:14) and Paul must have in mind his surrender of his body to all kinds of sufferings through which he would be able to 'boast' in a coming day. Yet even such Pauline self-giving for the furtherance of the gospel, unaccompanied by a life of love, is spiritually profitless.

The things Paul speaks of are good in themselves. We should seek spiritual gifts. We ought to give ourselves for the good of others and for the gospel. But love is indispensable – that love which is itself a response to God's love in Christ. Love is absolutely supreme and necessary. It alone is the true mark of spirituality, the essential sign of the Spirit's presence. Without it, one is not a Christian at all, and certainly not a spiritual one.

Questions
1. 'I am nothing.' Consider the relevance of this statement of Paul for yourself.
2. Does your fellowship look for gifted leaders or loving leaders? Paul suggests that a gifted leader without love would be useless. But would a loving person without the gift of leadership be fit to lead?
3. Why are the marks that non-Christians look for in the church so often absent?

1 Corinthians 13:4–7
Love's character

Paul paints a beautiful picture of the Christian life governed by love.

What does the love look like which Paul regards as so essential? Using fifteen well-chosen verbs, the apostle describes it by actions which unmistakably reflect the character of God in Christ.

As we look at the list we are, perhaps, reminded of Paul's own apostolic ministry in contrast to the attitude of some Corinthians towards him. But the passage reaches beyond this and is capable of the widest application.

Paul speaks of love as if it were a person (*Love is patient ... love is not rude*). He emphasizes that the person who displays love will show it by the presence or absence of these characteristics.

What is love like?
Paul begins with two positive characteristics which clearly reflect God's love to us in Christ (4 and see Romans 2:4). Patience means forbearance towards others, especially the endurance of injuries without retaliation. On the other hand, the word 'kind' points to active goodness in others' behalf, a readiness to pay back in kindness what has been received in hurt.

What love is not!
Next, Paul lists eight things which love is *not* (4b–6a) (the last being restated positively: 6b–7):

- *Envy.* The word 'envy' suggests that fellow believers should not be rivals for position or influence in the church, like, perhaps, some who stood against Paul as his rivals (4:18). It may also point to the

153

jealousy of those who did not have the more extraordinary gifts of the Corinthian 'charismatics' (to resort to the modern, incorrect use of the term: see 12:15, 16).

- *Boasting.* On the other hand, such 'charismatics' must learn not to brag (12:21). Or perhaps Paul's rivals are again in mind, claiming to possess wisdom (3:18) and knowledge (8:2) and, especially, to be spiritual (14:37). Such an attitude cannot have the good of the community at heart. So 'love does not boast'.

- *Proud.* In close connection with this, the word translated 'proud' refers to a 'windbag', to someone who is 'puffed up', arrogant. Paul has already applied this word to the Corinthians (4:6, 18; 5:2; 8:1).

- *Rude.* The person who loves does not ride roughshod over the feelings and sensitivities of the more vulnerable members of the church community. Many reputedly 'spiritual' people today have no idea how hurtful they can be in their careless and insensitive attitude to other people.

- *Self-seeking.* More fundamentally, loving Christians are not self-seeking (10:24, 33). They are even prepared to lay aside what they are entitled to – their 'rights' – pursuing the good of both neighbours and enemies (Philippians 2:4–11). This surely throws light on the whole discussion on spiritual gifts (see on chapter 14).

- *Easily angered.* The one who loves is not easily provoked to anger. Too many of us are touchy, almost waiting for someone to do something to us, real or imagined, at which to take offence. Just as God in Christ does not count our sins against us, so we are not to keep a file of personal grievances, bearing grudges and reacting in the light of such things when any fresh problem occurs. Christians are not only to have good memories. They are to have good forgetteries!

- *Delight in evil.* Paul adds: *love does not delight in evil* (6). For example, it does not grab at negatives (say, the failure of another believer or the faults of one's church) and, out of a supposed concern, continually raise the subject with people, eagerly feeding on it. On the contrary, it 'joins in rejoicing' on the side of behaviour that reflects the gospel ('truth'). The truly loving Christian, free from self-concern (and the need to justify self by gloating over the faults of others) can gladly and genuinely identify with the good and the righteousness of others, including those with whom he or she disagrees.

As has already been noted, certain Corinthian Christians thought they had arrived, that they were spiritually free in the fullest sense, and that all things were permitted to them (6:12). But Paul asserts here (7) that love always trusts, always hopes, always perseveres. In other words, these phrases imply that, in the here and now (for the 'then' has not yet arrived), love demands a voluntary restriction of personal freedom.

Only those who have the Holy Spirit can begin to fulfil the powerful description of love in verses 4–7, although some non-Christians may have virtues something like some of those listed here. It is a high standard, but the greatness of this Christ-like picture should inspire us to seek to conform increasingly to it. After all, even when we fail at many points, God's forgiveness is available (Psalm 130:4)

So, however much we have tried, and failed, to have a satisfactory relationship with a particular brother or sister, love demands that we keep on trying until either we win through or that person finally rejects us. 'Love always perseveres.'

Questions

1. Can you substitute your name in place of 'love' in verses 5 and 6? Think over the last few days and jot down any thoughts these verses prompt.
2. How far could verse 5 be said to be true of relationships in your church (especially between leaders and others and vice versa)?
3. 'See how these Christians love one another!' How far is this true today? Have things changed since New Testament times?

1 Corinthians 13:8–13
Love's permanence

Spiritual gifts remind us that the best is yet to come, and love is the breath of that life to come.

The statement *love never fails* (8) both looks back to what Paul has just written and reaches forward to verse 13 where he asserts that love (along with faith and hope) remains. In this final paragraph, the apostle returns to his overriding concern with spiritual gifts, although the theme of love is never far below the surface.

This paragraph contrasts the temporary and partial nature of the *charismata* and the permanence (and hence supremacy) of love. The Corinthians saw a particular spiritual gift as the essential mark of spirituality. Paul denies this; only love can be that! Such *charismata* were (simply) a means to the building up of the church in the present age (1:7).

Are the gifts still valid today?

Paul explains in verses 9 and 10 what he has said in verse 3. The gifts will eventually pass away *when perfection comes*. Some argue that 'perfection' refers to the time when the full revelation of the New Testament, the completion of the canon of Scripture (*i.e.* the Bible), occurs. On this view, the exercise of the extraordinary gifts was an immature stage in the life of the church and the need for such revelatory spiritual gifts has now passed; they accordingly ceased in the first or second century of the Christian era.

The completed Bible is, indeed, the final revelation of God, because God has spoken his 'last' word in his Son (Hebrews 1:2). No new revelation like that found in the Bible is to be expected today. However, this passage is not dealing with the completion of the canon. It is unlikely that Paul and especially the Corinthians would have understood the expression 'the perfect thing' to refer to the completed New Testament canon. Also, the verb used in verse 10 ('disappears') is used by Paul elsewhere to speak of the destruction, at Christ's second coming, of what belongs only to the present age (see 6:13; 15:24–26; 2 Thessalonians 2:8). Finally, *when perfection comes* must be a reference to the second coming of Christ because the 'now' and 'then' contrasts of verse 12, and the related expressions used there (*we shall see face to face*), plainly point to the end of the age.

This is not to say that all claims to possession of a particular charismatic gift are to be accepted, nor is it impossible that certain gifts should be withdrawn before the end. But they will all be unnecessary after Jesus' second coming. Certain Corinthians thought that they were already in heaven because they spoke in tongues. Paul tells them that this is precisely the evidence that they had *not* yet arrived there. For, when that which is complete comes, such things (whether tongues, prophecy or teaching) will be unnecessary.

Time to grow up

Paul now uses a standard form of contrast in the ancient world – that between an infant and an adult (11). In this way Paul admonishes the Corinthians for childishness (as he does in 14:20).

Behaviour appropriate to one period in one's life is inappropriate to another period, and in the same way spiritual gifts are inappropriate to the final stage of the church's existence.

Equally, spiritual gifts are appropriate to the present life of the church, just as the talk, thoughts and reasonings of childhood are appropriate during childhood. In addition, they are the activity of the Holy Spirit among God's people (12:7 and 11) and love itself promotes their use for the building up of the body during its present time of need (chapter 14:1ff.). However, the gifts are not for ever!

Corinth was well known in the ancient world as the producer of some of the finest bronze mirrors. This is probably why Paul speaks of this present age as the time when (literally) 'we look through (meaning "into") a mirror in a riddle' (12). He does not mean that present modes of revelation are mysterious, nor is he referring to the poor quality of these mirrors. (Recent research has suggested that they weren't too bad! In any case, such a suggestion could have been an affront to the Corinthians!) He is simply saying that the picture of reality given by a mirror is indirect. It is certainly incomplete (12). Wonderful as is the vision of God and his ways we obtain through prophecy and teaching, it is as nothing when compared with what we shall experience at the coming of Christ. At that time *we shall see face to face* will mean a direct manifestation of God to human beings. A modern comparison might be the difference between seeing a photograph of a person and seeing that person before us.

For us today, the *charismata* are a provision of God for the church's present existence, not to be dismissed as necessarily having ceased. But even these wonderful blessings are only a foretaste of the future. These very gifts remind us that we are still living in the 'not yet', whereas love (as described in 4–7) is the appearance of the eternal in time. When so-called 'charismatics' and 'non-charismatics' show love, not only among themselves but towards each other, then they are nearest to heaven!

Questions

1. How might you present the message of this chapter to another group, say a group of children?
2. How far could it be said that your fellowship is marked by faith, hope and love?
3. What are the differences between the world's view of love and that of this chapter? Have our churches got it right?

GETTING WORSHIP RIGHT
1 Corinthians 14:1–40

1 Corinthians 14:1–12
Building one another up

There is no point in speaking to people if they cannot understand what you are saying.

Paul's main concern here is that people will understand what is said in the gathered assembly if the church is to grow. This is why he argues that prophecy is a gift superior to tongues. In verses 1–19 he relates all this to the gathered believers and in verses 20–25 he relates it to unbelievers who come into the assembly.

Paul picks up the theme he introduced in 12:31a and now in verse 1 carries it forward under the impetus of chapter 13. Out of a life of 'love' the Corinthians are to seek the 'greater gifts', those which most readily build up the church community. As far as speech gifts are concerned, the understanding of the hearers is essential.

The command eagerly to desire spiritual gifts (here using the word the Corinthians preferred, so Paul may well be quoting again one of their slogans) is immediately qualified: 'but rather that you prophesy'.

Paul then gives the reasons (2–4). On the one hand, the gift of tongues edifies the speaker but not the church, because it is addressed to God and no-one understands the speaker. On the other hand, prophecy builds up the gathered congregation because it is addressed to people and speaks words which strengthen, encourage and comfort them. It is significant that Paul uses the word 'strengthening' (3) because it is the word usually translated 'edification'. This word emerges as the keynote of this chapter, just as love was the keynote of chapter 13.

Edification: building up the church

Paul does not condemn the self-edification that comes from uninterpreted tongues. His point is that 'in church' only what communicates to other believers through their minds is appropriate. However, it seems clear that Paul believed in a direct communing with God, by means of the Holy Spirit speaking through the human spirit, that sometimes bypassed the mind.

Paul summarizes what he has been saying by underlining his preference for prophecy over tongues in the assembly (5), and defines what he meant by the greater gifts in 12:31 in terms of the edification of the community.

The words *I would like every one of you to speak in tongues* (5) should no more be pressed than Paul's desire that all be single in 7:7! Paul simply desires that his converts enjoy as many good things as possible.

Paul is not opposing tongues, even in the assembly, but rather the use of uninterpreted tongues in church (5b). In verses 6–12 he supports his case with several illustrations.

The meaning of the illustrations in verses 7–9 is self-evident. In the case of both pleasure-giving musical instruments and the military horn, confusion of sounds and lack of clarity do not benefit the listener. Paul bluntly applies this: *so it is with you.* The point of the final illustration is that the hearer cannot understand tongues any more than he can understand someone speaking a foreign language, even though, in the latter case, the language has meaning to the speaker.

The words translated *Since you are eager to have spiritual gifts* (12) may be more literally translated 'since you are zealots for spirits'. The word 'spirits' appears to be Paul's way of speaking about the Holy Spirit manifesting himself through them as individuals (32 and 5:3, 4). Paul is, therefore, saying that the Corinthians have great zeal for their own spirits to be the mouthpiece of the Spirit, especially through speaking in tongues. For them this was the sure evidence of being spiritual. But the apostle wants them to build each other up through words that are understood.

Questions

1. What matters most to you, and why?
   - enjoying a sense of God's peace in private?
   - having a tremendous time worshipping with others?
   - helping someone else take a step forward with God?
2. How deeply should we expect to know one another as Christians? How do we deepen our fellowship: by speech only or by other means (e.g. silence, communion, shared experience)?
3. Do non-Christians sometimes find the church 'foreign'? What might we do about this?

1 Corinthians 14:13–19

Keep it clear!

Whatever may take place in an individual's private spiritual life, congregational worship is a place for clear and understandable ministry.

 What effect does it have on a worship meeting when someone speaks in an unknown tongue? Drawing upon his own experience, Paul underlines a basic principle. Whenever he prayed in tongues, he prayed in his spirit (through the Spirit), but it did not benefit either his mind or those of his hearers (13, 14).

Paul does not intend to stop praying, or even singing, in tongues (or 'in the Spirit' as he calls it here, perhaps using the Corinthians' description of tongues-speaking) but, when meeting with others, he will pray and sing in a way which is understood (15, 16). This almost seems to relegate tongues-speaking to private devotions.

He then applies this to the Corinthians (16, 17). Their worship is to be understandable and a means to build others up. It is not a place for private religious experience.

With a further personal testimony (18, 19), Paul makes his concluding point. He gives the Corinthians a glimpse of his own spirituality (perhaps ironically, saying, *I speak in tongues more than all you*). Presumably, this would have been an unexpected shock to the 'spiritual' Corinthians but does affirm in the strongest terms the gift which preoccupied them. However, he does this precisely so that he can contradict their thinking about what should take place in the assembly.

Paul obviously means that he exercised his remarkable gift of tongues in private. It is just as clear that to indulge this gift without interpretation 'in church' (referring to the actual gathering together of God's people) would be entirely inappropriate. In terms reminiscent of verse 15 (*five intelligible words* is literally 'five words with my mind': 19)

Paul underlines that the assembled church is a place where everything should be clearly understood.

Questions
1. How should the gift of tongues be regarded in the life of the church, in services and in house groups?
2. The Corinthians judged other people's spirituality by outward 'evidences'. Paul did too (see chapter 13). What were these evidences? What should our church learn from the major differences between the two?

1 Corinthians 14:20–25
Watch out! Unbelievers about!

Church members should be concerned not only about their own upbuilding but about that of visiting unbelievers too.

In verses 20–25 Paul extends the principle that people need to understand one another. Unbelievers who are present in church gatherings also need to know what is going on!

The childishness Paul criticizes here (20) does not relate to the use of tongues as such, but to the pedestal on which the Corinthians had set them. They regarded it as the mark of their new superior spirituality, yet their behaviour left much to be desired.

Paul seems to imply here that the Corinthians were in danger of playing the same role as the 'children' referred to by the mockers of the prophet in Isaiah 28:9, 10 – children who rejected the word of the Lord.

Paul quotes verses 11 and 12 from the same chapter. His quotation can be translated:

> With other tongues
>> and through the lips of others
> I will speak to this people,
>> but even then they will not obey me. (21)

In Isaiah, 'speaking in tongues' by foreigners (Assyrians) did not produce belief. In fact, it both led to and was part of Israel's judgment, for the Assyrians were actually an invading army. Paul modifies the end of the quote to emphasize the fact that tongues do not lead sinners to obedience.

The Corinthians took tongues as a 'sign' of God's special blessing and presence. 'Not so,' says Paul (22a). They are not evidence of being spiritual or of the presence of God in church. In fact, in the light of verse 21, the 'sign' becomes something negative, working to the disadvantage of unbelievers. Paul expands this point in verse 23 by showing that tongues, as abused by the Corinthians in their church gatherings, function in this way, bringing unbelievers under judgment. Because what is happening in the assembly is not understood, unbelievers receive no message from God. They see the work of the Spirit as madness and, contrary to God's intention, they are brought under judgment.

Paul shows (by a further picture of a Christian assembly: 22b) that prophecy which can be understood by all and which reveals God's purpose is a sign of God's approval. When the unbeliever falls down and exclaims, *God is really among you!* (the climax to this passage), it is a 'sign' for believers; it is the indication of God's favour resting upon them.

In verses 24b and 25a we read of the deep, probing work of the Holy Spirit in people's lives in the here and now, which anticipates the final judgment. The words of verse 25b point to conversion, especially in the light of their Old Testament background (see Isaiah 45:14 and Zechariah 8:23). All this amounts to a sure sign of the presence of God in the believing community. No wonder the gift of tongues was more popular with the Corinthians! It was relatively insignificant compared with the great works of God which Paul is describing.

Questions

1. How important are our minds for our growth as Christians? Can our minds hinder our growing closer to God?
2. Churches today sometimes find strange behaviour taking place. Some think the Spirit is at work, others that madness has taken hold of the people of God. How can we distinguish between God's work and madness?

Prophecy and preaching

'Tongues are unclear, prophecy isn't – so I prefer prophecy in church!' This summarizes Paul's message in this section. But what exactly is 'prophecy'?

Opinions differ. Some suggest that it is basically preaching, because preaching attempts to make God's word as clear as possible. Others, however, understand prophecy as special words of direct revelation given by God to a church or to individuals, through an 'anointed' person.

Which view is right? In deciding this issue, these are the things to bear in mind:

165

- In the Old Testament, a prophet is someone who speaks from God to his people. This helps us to define what a prophet is. How prophets received the message from God seems to have varied. Sometimes it involved very careful thought and composition, sometimes it was given 'directly'.

- 'Preaching' is not a specific spiritual gift in 1 Corinthians. When Paul refers to it (1:23; 2:4) he uses a general word which means 'proclaim'.

- In his list of gifts in 12:28, Paul distinguishes between prophets and teachers. Teachers would certainly have 'proclaimed' or 'preached'. In Ephesians 4:11 prophets are included in a list of five ministries, all of which could appropriately be exercised through preaching (and in other ways): those of apostles, prophets, evangelists, pastors and teachers.

- Undoubtedly all those who stood up to speak to the church in Corinth – whether prophets, teachers, pastors, or whatever – hoped and prayed that their words would be the word of the Lord to the church. So anyone who spoke a spot-on word from God could be said to have 'prophesied'. Of course, some were already convinced that they were speaking God's word, even before they saw the effect on the church. But even in their case, the rest of the church had to 'weigh' what was said (14:29), that is, decide whether it really was from God, and what the response should be.

- But even if anyone at all could speak a word from God like this, Paul uses the word 'prophesy' in connection with receiving revelation direct from God (14:29–30).

166

1 Corinthians 14:26–33
Keeping order

A church is built upon ministries that are understood and an ordered community.

Paul now returns to the subject which concerned him in chapter 12; that each person should have the opportunity to minister to the body, the church. He re-emphasizes the point made in the present chapter that these ministries have their purpose in the edification of the church (26).

Paul refers to various contributions that worshippers might make in a service (without suggesting that the list is complete). He is writing in a very specific situation and the passage is not intended to offer us a rule book. We need to ask how the principles might apply to the various situations we encounter today.

Tongues

Paul has been concerned to emphasize that the Spirit's gifts bring clear understanding. Now the spotlight shifts and we see that the gifts need an orderly structure to enable them to be used to build up the church (27, 28). Such a framework is not the same as a rigid pattern of worship. It does not deny spontaneity or variety, as this passage itself makes clear (30, 31). On the other hand, what Paul writes here (as confirmed by 32, 33) marks off the Christian assembly from a forum of pagan ecstasy. Christian inspiration never leads to people being 'out of control', or to the chaos that apparently tended to reign at Corinth (23). It is assumed that those with authentic spiritual gifts are well able to use them in an orderly way.

By these instructions, Paul carefully ensures that Christian assemblies are not dominated by such phenomena as tongues, as was apparently the case at Corinth. Indeed, this gift should not be used at all in the assembly if there is no-one present who can give a clear, edifying interpretation. If there is none, the tongues-speaker should use her or his gift privately.

Some suggest that the words 'to himself' mean 'at home'. Whether or not this is the case it does seem that Paul regarded this spiritual gift as largely for private use.

Prophecy

Paul proceeds to give parallel guidelines for the use of the gift of prophecy (29–31). No more than two or three should speak before the appropriate evaluation takes place. In the case of tongues, Paul had implied that 'at the most' (27) two or three should speak in the whole meeting. This difference should be noted.

Notice that Paul did not apparently expect there to be 'official' tongues-interpreters or prophets. The tongue might be interpreted by the speaker (13) or 'someone' else in the assembly (27). The prophets were simply members of the congregation who exercised the gift of prophecy. Potentially, this could be any believer (31, and compare verse 24).

In practice, of course, certain people would tend to exercise certain ministries (see Romans 12:6–8). However, this does not alter the principle, well stated by one writer, that 'any member of the body can be used at any meeting to bring any gift'. In this respect the 'others' who are to weigh carefully what is said are probably the rest of the gathered assembly. Each one is responsible to test everything (see 1 Thessalonians 5:19–22). While we are to be open to God's Word (as this whole paragraph on prophecy implies), we are neither to be gullible nor to charge such people as pastors with the whole responsibility of our spiritual direction and well-being. We must all play a responsible part in whatever is done.

The weighing carefully or 'discerning' is probably not a question of testing whether the one prophesying is speaking by a foreign spirit (as in 1 John 4:1), but of evaluating to what degree a given prophecy really conforms to the Spirit of God (see 12:10), which may point to that which is consistent with faith in Jesus Christ. Such prophecies given in worship are for the church to receive intelligently and to agree upon. They are not so much a word of foresight about an individual, church or nation but a means of 'instruction' or 'encouragement'. This must mean that they are closely related to that 'Word of God' which is the gospel of Jesus Christ (see 1 Thessalonians 2:11–13).

The *spirits of prophets* (32) points to the Spirit of God speaking through the spirit of each prophet (see 12:10 and compare 5:3, 4 and 14:12, 14–15). Because when God's Spirit is at work those taking part keep their self-control, tongues-speakers can contribute one at a time (27), together with the prophets they can be silent when necessary (28, 30) and believers can prophesy in turn (31). The inspiration present in a Christian assembly is radically different from the uncontrolled ecstasy of those pagan cults which were apparently having too much influence in what took place in the church in Corinth.

The 'atmosphere' of Christian gatherings has its basis in the character of God. Over against the disorder and mania which characterize the worship of pagan deities, the character of God is such that his worship does not bring confusion but rather that harmony in the Spirit consistent with the controlling purpose of edifying the church (26). It also promotes the wholesome blessing of all who attend. Such is 'peace'.

The principle that emerges is well stated by one commentator: 'The character of one's deity is reflected in the character of one's worship.' The application of this to the situation at Corinth is clear enough. However, perhaps its application to some churches today (see on 26) would promote more spontaneity and joy in rather stiff and sombre gatherings.

Questions

1. What would Paul think of a worship meeting where many of those present appear to be 'spaced out' and almost unconscious of those around them?
2. Some churches have 'liturgical' worship, following a set, written form of prayer. Are there dangers or advantages in this? What would Paul say, in the light of his teaching here?
3. What sort of God does my worship, or the worship of my church, reflect? What aspects of his character are we not adequately reflecting?

1 Corinthians 14:34–40
Self-sufficient worship

Paul confronts the controversial question concerning women taking part in meetings. At the same time he challenges once again the Corinthians' views on spirituality.

Verses 34 and 35 do not obviously seem to fit at this point and they may be an aside dealing with another matter relating to order in the church gatherings (but see 'Women in worship', p. 171). Paul seems to be dealing with interruptions in the assemblies by certain women, primarily married ones, who were abusing their new-found liberty in Christ (see chapter 7 and 11:2–16). It seems that these women were asking disruptive questions during 'worship', perhaps with raised voices, and possibly about what was being said in a tongue or prophecy. Such a practice was not fitting (11:13). It is this that Paul prohibits.

Looking back over all that he has said in this chapter, Paul gets down to basics (36–38). What right have the Corinthians to be different from other churches? Do they have a unique hotline to God? The implied answer is 'No'. Since this is the case he commands them to keep in line and encourage understandable and orderly worship as the other churches do.

We need to beware of the self-sufficient tendency that Paul exposes here. Criticisms of church unity, other denominations, and 'traditional' Christianity are sometimes expressed in terms that seem to imply that the critics alone take the Bible seriously. In the light of this letter it is doubtful whether this would be Paul's perspective.

He is saying here that truly spiritual people (especially those who also rank themselves as 'prophets' in some official sense) will recognize his apostolic authority and perceive the Lord Jesus as the source of all that Paul has been writing about the worship meetings of the church. In other words, those who really are spiritual persons will recognize and submit to the word of Christ – a reality which we ought to take seriously today! Indeed, in verse 38, Paul pronounces a prophetic sentence of judgment on those who fail to do this.

With the significant 'therefore' (or 'so then'), Paul signals the summary of all that he has been saying in this chapter (39, 40):

- First, he repeats the call with which he began: 'Be eager to prophesy.'

- Second, he permits the presence of tongues, under the conditions he has previously described.

- Third, he summarizes his concluding guidelines on order. The love that longs to build up ought to promote a living assembly of harmony and beauty which will, in turn, attract outsiders.

Questions
1. In verses 33 and 36 Paul gives the Corinthians encouragement to match their practices to those of other churches. Should all our churches basically worship alike? When do differences become wrong divergences?
2. The teaching here on the place of women in the church has caused heartache and difficulty. Why? How do you think you or your church should respond? Remember to discuss this with sensitivity (and see the section 'Women in worship' below).
3. How can we promote order in 'worship' without undermining freedom and spontaneity?

Women in worship
The long-held view that verses 34–35 prohibit all women from speaking in any public worship simply will not work! It does not fit with what Paul writes in 11:2–16 (see discussion on that passage) and makes his repeated use of *all* and *everybody* in this chapter (compare *everybody is prophesying*, verse 24, and *For you can all prophesy in turn*, verse 31) seem rather hollow, to say the least.

Among other views recently suggested by conservative evangelical scholars are the following:

1. Paul is excluding women from the evaluating and discerning of prophecies mentioned in verse 29. This latter is taken as a more

authoritative act than prophetic speech itself and thus is inappropriate for a woman (wife) in church. This is an ingenious view, but it is difficult to see how the Corinthians would have understood the words of verses 34 and 35 in this way, given their distance from verse 29.

2. It must be admitted that these words do not sound very much like Paul and therefore it has been suggested either that they are not authentic (on the basis of variations in the Greek manuscripts that do indeed exist) or that they are another quotation by Paul of the words of certain Jewish Christians at Corinth which Paul then rebuffs in verse 36 (where it is possible to translate the Greek word at the beginning of the verse as 'Nonsense').

There may be those who plead for what they would call the 'plain meaning of the text', but honesty requires that we admit the existence of problems with all the views which have been advocated up to now (including the view tentatively adopted by the authors of this book!). We ought to acknowledge that our own cultural and temperamental prejudices can sometimes influence our reading of Scripture more than we realize.

An example of this could be that British evangelicals might criticize Latin American believers of undermining the authority of the Scriptures because women often exercise ministries of public teaching and even leadership in their churches. However, most Latin American evangelicals take a high view of Scripture and they might well feel that many British evangelical Christians do not take the New Testament's emphasis on spiritual warfare and demonic activity seriously enough!

13

THE RESURRECTION OF BELIEVERS
1 Corinthians 15:1–58

1 Corinthians 15:1–11
The resurrection of Christ

Paul takes up a new and highly important theme – the resurrection of believers. Its basis is the resurrection of Christ as an objective fact.

 Although this chapter deals with a new theme, we ought not to separate it too much from chapters 12–14, since Paul appears to be confronting the same error again (see 'Celestial resurrection', p. 118) The Corinthians regarded themselves as having already risen (perhaps in their baptism) to enter the true 'spirituality' (*cf.* 2 Timothy 2:17–18), so that life was essentially an experience of 'spirit'. Not only did they see a future physical resurrection as unnecessary but, under the influence of Greek philosophy (see discussion on chapter 1), it is likely that they viewed the body as something inferior, to be happily left behind at death.

Paul begins his response to this, in verses 1–11, by reminding his readers of what they had already accepted in theory: that Jesus Christ truly rose physically from a real state of death. Secondly, in verses 12–34, he shows how illogical was the denial of the bodily resurrection of believers. Thirdly, in verses 35–58, responding to a misdirected scepticism, he affirms the form in which believers are raised, that is, in a body adapted to the glorious conditions of the future.

Paul starts by reminding the Corinthians of what they appeared to have forgotten. The gospel, the good news of their past, present and future salvation, was the basic fact on which their very lives depended. But if there was no resurrection, that very gospel would be fatally wrecked and their 'belief' would be a belief in nothing ('in vain').

What is this gospel to which he has referred? Paul makes that clear in verses 3–5, using Jewish technical language for religious instruction and probably using a creed of the early church (see 'Creeds', p. 176).

The creed emphasizes the vital importance of atonement in the Christian 'tradition'. Christ died on behalf of others to satisfy the penalty of sin and to overcome the yawning gap between God and human beings on account of human sinfulness (11:23–25 and Isaiah 53). Above all, this confession points to the reality of the resurrection of a dead corpse rather than a merely 'spiritual' renewal of some sort. Christ not only 'died'; he was 'buried'. Not only 'was he raised' (implication: God did it); it was a genuine resurrection whereby *he appeared to* or 'was seen by' various individuals and groups. Paul refers specifically here to 'the Twelve', a title for the unique group of original apostles.

The linking of the words *according to the Scriptures* with the resurrection of Christ *on the third day*, probably suggests that the Old Testament as a whole (see Psalms 16:8–11 and 110:1) bears witness to the Messiah's resurrection, a variety of texts suggesting that vindication took place on the third day (see Hosea 6:2; Jonah 1:17; and Matthew 12:40).

For the Jews there was but one resurrection, the general resurrection. So if the tradition indicated that one man had been raised, an event confirmed by his appearances, then the general resurrection had begun. In other words, to establish that Christ had been raised is to establish the fact of the resurrection from the dead.

Paul then piles up further evidence for the resurrection (6–8). Obviously, the experience *at the same time* (6) of the crowd, most of whom were still 'available for comment', could not be easily dismissed. He also mentions James, the brother of the Lord, who after his earlier unbelief became a leader of the church in Jerusalem (see John 7:2–9, Galatians 1:19 and Acts 15:13ff.) and 'all the apostles', probably referring to the entire group who came to be known as apostles (including, but going beyond, 'the Twelve': Acts 1:6–11).

This last reference leads Paul to mention himself. The word translated as *one abnormally born* (8) points to some form of premature birth and was perhaps a term of disparagement used by the Corinthians towards him. What a way to treat one who utterly gave himself for them (*cf.* 4:15)!

So Paul mentions his fruitful ministry among them, showing that what they saw as his weakness and even freakishness was the true evidence of the grace of God in his life (*cf.* 4:9–13 and 2 Corinthians 10 – 13). Paul was no super-charged adherent of the personality cult – a point that should not be missed today.

Paul shows us here what grace really means. He knew that in his former persecuting zeal he really had been the chief of sinners (1 Timothy

1:13–16). Not only his salvation, but even his apostleship, was undeserved! Grace was not merely for the benefit of the apostle, to warm his heart. It worked in practice and the Corinthian church was one of the results. His very response to God's grace ('I worked': verse 10) was a part of that work of God's grace. This is a mystery but a glorious truth.

The gospel embraced by all true believers has no meaning apart from the bodily resurrection of Christ. On this foundation, Paul will construct his argument in the rest of the chapter.

In the light of what Paul is saying it looks as if those who deny the bodily resurrection of Christ are really denying the Christian faith. The passage does not *prove* Christ's resurrection. This can only be received as an article of faith. However, it *confirms* that it is and must remain an article of the church's faith and, at the same time, it calls the church to proclaim this resurrection and salvation through the whole work of Christ.

Questions
1. Why do you think that Jesus no longer appears to us today as he did to the eyewitnesses (5–8)?
2. Is it possible to 'believe in vain' (2)? How can you encourage people who fear that they might have fallen into this trap?
3. Verses 1–5 contain a kind of early 'creed'. How important are Christian creeds (see 'Creeds' below)? What part should they play in our lives and worship?

Creeds

One of the earliest examples of a creed or brief statement of Christian faith is recorded in 1 Corinthians 15:3–5. Creeds have played an important role in the history of the church, some being very ancient indeed. The 'Apostles' Creed' goes back to the third century and the 'Nicene Creed' (still said in many churches at communion services) dates back to a church council in AD 381.

Paul tells us the purpose of creeds in 15:3: *For what I received I passed on to you as of first importance.* Creeds involve deciding what is really the heart of the Christian faith, what we simply cannot do without. Christians can and do disagree about many things, but creeds attempt to define essentials, the supremely important things without which true faith is impossible. Paul thought the Corinthians were throwing away an essential by not believing in the physical resurrection of Jesus.

1 Corinthians 15:12–19
What if Christ did not rise?

Paul shows, irresistibly, the awful consequences of the Corinthian denial of the future bodily resurrection of believers.

 Some influential Corinthians (see 4:18; 9:3) denied the future bodily resurrection of believers (12, 13). Paul exposes the illogicality of their position and the terrible consequences it would have (if it were true) both now and in the future, for both him and them. If there is no such thing as resurrection then Christ was not raised.

So what if Christ did not rise? 'Both our preaching and your believing have no real basis,' says Paul (14). Faith is not some mystical quality to carry us through life. It has meaning only if it is based on fact, the fact of the resurrection of Christ.

Paul presses home the appalling logical outcome of their position (that is, Christ did not rise), by showing how useless the apostolic preaching would have been if the false teachers were right. The long and the short of it is that this preaching turns out to be a lie, a lie that ultimately implicates God himself. 'We have witnessed against God,' says Paul, or so we could translate it. It might come as a shock to us to realize that we too could be in danger of opposing God if our ideas are not founded on the Bible.

Paul turns now to the uselessness of the Corinthians' faith if there is no resurrection (17–18). With regard to the living, they are still in their sins. The point is, on their view, God has not set his seal on the work of his Son by raising him (15) and therefore his death has not satisfied the penalty of sin (3); there is neither justification (being made right with God) nor sanctification (increasing holiness of life) (see 6:11; Romans 4:25; 5:10). By denying their future resurrection, the Corinthians have (in principle) destroyed both their past and their present (1, 2).

With regard to those believers who are already dead (*i.e.*, 'those who have fallen asleep in Christ', *cf.* 11:30), they have perished. This is because when they died, they were like the living of verse 17, still in their sins. No forgiveness for their sins was available. In other words, if the Corinthian position over the bodily resurrection of believers were true, far from having already 'arrived', there would be neither a past, a present, nor a future for Christians.

Is Christianity, as some say, an 'opiate of the people', a drug to blot out a hopeless present and a ghastly future? No. Christ gives us a new life now and a bright hope for the future. But if Christ is not raised from the dead (17), we have, in reality, neither forgiveness in the present nor hope for the future. We are miserable indeed!

After reflecting on the awful consequences if the resurrection of Christ did not happen, it comes as a tremendous relief to us to realize afresh that the opposite is the case! This is what Paul wants us to see and what he goes on to underline in the following passage.

Questions
1. You have the task of leading an 'Agnostics Anonymous' session on the resurrection of Jesus. What arguments would you use to show that he really rose from the dead?
2. Some church leaders, especially in Britain and the United States, have caused a stir by saying that they do not believe in a physical resurrection but, rather, in a spiritual resurrection; the disciples experienced the continuing 'livingness' of Jesus. What would your comments be?
3. Do you have to believe in the physical resurrection of Jesus to become a Christian? If so, how can we bring the materialistic and rationalistic person to faith today?

1 Corinthians 15:20–34
But he did rise! Hallelujah!

Thank God that what Paul had just written in verses 12–19 was hypothetical! Paul now affirms the certainty of the resurrection of the dead with some earthy arguments.

At this point Paul leads us out of a dark tunnel of despair back into bright sunshine. In reality Christ *did* rise (20). The Corinthians had, in principle, believed it and what he wrote in verses 1–11 confirms the objective reality of what they had received.

Those in Christ who have fallen asleep (18) are not 'lost', but are destined for resurrection. Indeed, as this passage goes on to show (20–28), Christ's resurrection has started the overthrow of death itself and the very character of God requires the complete fulfilment of this process.

The key word in verse 20 is 'firstfruits'. In Old Testament times, the firstfruits of the harvest were offered to God (Leviticus 23:9–14). But here Paul means that the first part of the harvest is a guarantee of the full harvest to come. Since Christ is God's 'firstfruits', the resurrection of the believing dead has been guaranteed by God himself, so the full harvest is absolutely inevitable.

To explain this idea Paul uses for the first time the Adam–Christ illustration (21, 22) which he takes up again in a different way in verses 45–49 (and see Romans 5:12–21). Adam and Christ are seen as the heads of two humanities, the old and the new. Just as death is the inevitable common lot of human beings because they share in the humanity and sinfulness of the one man, Adam, those who belong to the new humanity by grace (that is, they are 'in Christ') will just as inevitably be raised from the dead. They will share in the life of the Risen One.

179

Death: the last enemy
However, contrary to the viewpoint of 'some' among the Corinthians, salvation does not happen all at once, in the here and now. Despite Christ's resurrection, believers still die. In the realm of the kingdom of God, there is not only an 'already' (consistent with the fact that Christ 'has been raised from the dead'), there is also a 'not yet' (a future reality whose timing is not known).

In God's scheme of things the pattern is as follows (23, 24): first, there is Christ's resurrection as 'firstfruits'; then, as a result of this, there is the resurrection of the dead who belong to him, at his coming or *parousia* (his glorious arrival). At this time (Paul literally says, 'then the end') *the end will come*. The goal or fulfilment of all that has gone before will be reached. Christ will have finally overthrown *all dominion, authority and power* (especially death), and secondly, he will therefore turn over his authority to God the Father.

It is clear then that between the resurrection (and ascension) of Christ and his glorious return is the time of his reign. This must continue until the destruction of death (25–27). Paul offers his own interpretation of Psalms 110:1 and 8:6 to support his claim.

In case the glorious appeal of verses 20–28 has not fully found its mark, Paul comes down to earth in verses 29–34, and shows how the Corinthians' daily lives would not make sense if there were no resurrection of the dead. He concludes the entire section with a strong call to them to make a new beginning (29).

Living in the light of the resurrection
Since there are so many different interpretations of the meaning of verse 29 (one writer indicates that there are at least forty different solutions, another refers to the existence of up to two hundred!) and we do not know what the situation was, we cannot offer a very confident explanation. But it looks as if the apostle is speaking of the baptism of one person as the representative of another. Paul does not approve this practice, but neither does he seem to regard it as such a serious fault. It appears to have been the eccentric practice of only a few at Corinth and may indicate that some believers were being baptized for other believers who suddenly died (11:30) and had not yet been baptized. What is clear is Paul's emphasis on the inconsistency, indeed, the absurdity, of this practice among them if there is no resurrection of the dead and therefore (in line with what he has shown already) no future for those who have died.

Paul then returns to his own weaknesses and sufferings (30–32), which appear to have been a butt of the Corinthians' criticism in the light of their idea of (super-)spirituality. He perhaps implies that if they were right about there being no resurrection, then they are also right to doubt his apostleship. In reality, they were wrong about both. The main point here is that Paul's labours as an apostle were absurd if there were no resurrection and therefore neither forgiveness of sins in the present nor solid hope for the future (see discussion on verses 12–19).

Paul stresses that he faces the reality of death every day. In this respect, the 'wild beasts' he fought with in Ephesus (from where he sent this letter) probably refer to the human opposition and even physical dangers which he faced there (16:8–9). Such a death-confronting life of daily dying would have no point if there were no resurrection, with all that this implies. One might as well live the despairing, dissolute life reflected in the quote from Isaiah 22:13 (32). Does one detect something of the Corinthians' own lifestyle in these words?

What the Corinthians believed affected how they lived (33, 34). Could it be that their denial of the resurrection was directly linked to many of the behavioural problems corrected by this letter? The word translated as 'company' can also mean 'conversations' such as those that deny the resurrection of the dead.

The final two appeals certainly suggest that their denial of the bodily resurrection of believers undermined their behaviour. They must snap out of their present state of delusion and stop the sinning they were presently engaged in. These so-called 'spiritual ones' among them, enlightened with a supposed superior wisdom and knowledge, were in fact, like the surrounding pagans, 'ignorant' of the God who stands behind Christ's resurrection, the consequent destruction of death and all that is associated with it. Oh that they might all be shamed into a change of thinking and behaviour!

Christ's resurrection has started a chain of inevitable events that secures both our present and our future. This should affect the way we currently live, even in the midst of weakness and sufferings. There is a real relationship between what one believes about the future and how one lives in the present, precisely because it is all bound up with the nature and character of God himself.

Questions
1. How has this passage helped your faith?
2. How should the reality of the resurrection, as expounded here by Paul, affect the life and the worship of your church?
3. What are the 'powers, dominions and authorities' yet to be destroyed by Jesus (24)? Must we wait for him to do this or can we help?

1 Corinthians 15:35–49
With what kind of body will we rise?

Paul answers questions about the resurrection of the body with illustrations from creation and then by a return to the Adam–Christ comparison. He points to the glorious, heavenly existence which is the destiny of believers through the risen, glorified Christ.

 It is probable that the two questions in verse 35 are not separate questions but that the second explains the first. The 'How?' of the resurrection relates to the kind of body with which the dead will rise. This was apparently a stock expression of scepticism about a future resurrection in the Mediterranean world of the day (see Luke 20:29–33), and probably shows the root of the Corinthians' problem in this area. They were thinking merely of corpses coming to life.

Paul responds to this with two sets of homely pictures, that of seeds (36–38) and that of different kinds of bodies (39–41). He then applies these principles to the future resurrection of the dead (42–44). This doctrine is not so 'way out' after all! However, it is something beyond all expectation and so he further illustrates what he has been showing by picking up the Adam–Christ comparison from verses 21–22 (45–49). The key to everything is the resurrection of Jesus Christ and his glorious transformation.

Seeds
'What kind of body shall we have?' is the question of a fool (36). A 'fool', in the Old Testament sense, is a person who has failed to take God into account (all this was contrary to the Corinthians' image of themselves!). 'You have the answer in your own hands', says Paul –

they only had to look at what God had arranged in the everyday world of plant life.

The world of plant life shows that out of death a new form of life bursts forth (37). There is continuity: the 'body' (the plant or crop) that comes into being emerges from the seed that was sown. There is also discontinuity: the life that comes forth does so in a transformed 'body' very different from the seed (38). Above all, God is behind all this.

Bodies

God has ordered his creation so that there are many kinds of bodies, each one adapted to its own mode of existence. So it is reasonable (within the context of faith) to expect a resurrection body which is adapted to the heavenly mode of existence.

In verse 40 Paul mentions 'heavenly bodies' and 'earthly bodies'. The earthly bodies refer to animal life (39, and see Genesis 1:20, 24, 26). The heavenly bodies, expressed in terms of 'splendour', are those listed in verse 41; sun, moon and stars. The word translated as 'splendour' is the word for 'glory' (43) and clearly anticipates the development of Paul's argument.

The principles applied

Here then we have two pictures: one emphasizing that the future body will be continuous with the present one but changed (like a seed and a plant); the other that we shall be different from one another (like sun, moon and stars). Paul uses four contrasts to make his point (42, 43):

- The body is sown (dies) perishable but rises never more to decay, an act of God which the Corinthians had not reckoned with.

- It is sown in human dishonour and raised in divine glory (see Philippians 3:21).

- It is sown in weakness (not the 'super-spirituality' of the Corinthians) and raised in God's power.

- It is sown as a natural, physical body and raised as a supernatural body, not a wisp of cloudy gas but a solid body fitted for a spiritual life with God.

The Corinthians would have been shocked by Paul's linking of the words 'spiritual' and 'body'. But he punches his argument home: 'If there is a natural body, there is also a spiritual body.' To help them he returns to the Adam–Christ comparison.

1 Corinthians: Crossway Bible Guide

Adam and Christ

Adam and Christ are seen as representatives of the two kinds of body mentioned in verse 44. The word 'being' used of Adam (in Genesis 2:7) relates to the word 'natural' (as in 'natural body') in verse 44, and the word used here to describe Christ (related to the word 'spiritual') emerges from the words, 'and he breathed into his face the breath of life', in the old Greek version. In addition, the word translated 'life-giving' suggests resurrection (45).

The 'spiritual ones' at Corinth thought they had already 'arrived' and that the body could be discounted. Paul shows the need to take account of the bodily side of their present life in the Spirit (46), for they had not yet obtained that full spirituality which includes a transformed body fitted for last-age existence. They must wait for the 'after that'!

Linking verses 47 and 48 with verse 45, we can now grasp clearly the line of thought. The first Adam was given a 'natural body' at creation, a body subject to decay and death. This Adam in fact brought death into the world, affecting the whole of that humanity of which he became the representative (22a). On the other hand, the last Adam, who received a 'spiritual (supernatural, or glorified) body' at his resurrection, became the actual source of both spiritual life and the spiritual body (the kind of body we will have at the resurrection) for that humanity of which he became the representative. How tremendous this is!

The result of all this is a glorious hope (49). With what kind of body will the dead (in Christ) be raised? Answer: *we shall bear the likeness of the man from heaven* (or heavenly man).

Some suggest the alternative translation: 'so let us bear the likeness of the man from heaven'. If this is correct, Christians are being urged to conform to the life of 'the heavenly man' here and now as they await that glorious day when they shall do so fully (see 50–58). Is Paul perhaps implying that 'you will never be fully "spiritual" at all if you do not conform to Christ in the present'? Paul frequently comes back to matters of behaviour, how our beliefs change our lives (see 33, 34 and 58).

We may not be able to grasp clearly what Paul means by 'a spiritual body', but it is a tremendous and encouraging thought that Jesus Christ – as the Risen One – is the source and guarantee of our resurrection bodies and that they will be patterned after his. For Paul, 'full spirituality' is not a present experience, despite what some people try to teach us today. It is to bear the likeness of Christ in a transformed body fitted for the eternal age to come.

Questions
1. What part does your body play in your present life in the Spirit?
2. Basing your thoughts on this passage, write a 'letter of consolation' to a friend whose father has just died.
3. In the light of this passage, how should we deal with scepticism in the church about resurrection?

1 Corinthians 15:50–58
Tremendous transformation

Our bodies need to change in order to enter the heavenly existence of the age to come. That existence is certain on the basis of what Jesus Christ has done. As usual this has earthly implications.

Paul sums up his argument. His point all along has been that the 'body that shall be' is a transformed version of the one that was 'sown' (36–38). Without that change the body cannot inherit the future, heavenly mode of existence of 47–49, called here *the kingdom of God* (50; see also 24 and 6:9).

The last trumpet

Over against this reality, there is a 'mystery', something once hidden but now revealed in Christ (51). This mystery is not that of the bodiless immortality favoured among the Corinthians. Rather, it means that all, including those who are alive at the time of Christ's coming, must be transformed so that they have imperishable bodies, conformed to the likeness of the heavenly man.

But what a shock this 'mystery' would have been among those Corinthians who thought they had already 'arrived' spiritually (see 4:8), that they needed nothing more and that the body is irrelevant. Even the living would have to be changed – a change affecting their very bodies – in order truly to arrive!

This change will happen as a split-second transformation (52), occurring at the coming of Christ (see also 1 Thessalonians 4:13–17). It will be inaugurated by 'the last trumpet', an Old Testament picture in which it signals the end (see Isaiah 27:13 for an example).

The sounding of this trumpet (1 Thessalonians 4:16) heralds both the resurrection of the dead (with changed bodies) and the transformation of the living ('we'). It seems that all these events occur at precisely the same time.

Paul concludes here by underlining that it is God's decision that the living and the dead have transformed bodies in order to enter the heavenly mode of existence. Through the last Adam there is an assured end to the decay and death that stems from the first Adam. It is precisely this abolition of death itself, through the resurrection and transformation that will take place at the coming of Christ, that Paul powerfully and eloquently asserts here (54, 55). This is exactly in line with what he had argued in verses 23–28, only here there is a note of exaltation and triumph.

The abolition of death and its consequences

Paul now quotes two Old Testament texts which he sees as fulfilled in Christ but which have not yet taken place. He first cites Isaiah 25:8 but uses the word 'victory' instead of 'for ever'. Paul proceeds to include the same word in his quotation from Hosea 13:14 and then repeats it in verse 57.

What we have here then is a powerful taunt of death. On the one hand, Paul sees the glorious future as if it were already here because Christ's own death and resurrection set the process going. On the other hand, he can speak in the present tense precisely because, in Christ, the End has already begun. The 'already' and the 'not yet' are not one (as they had become to the Corinthians), but they are inseparably linked!

The apostle then gives a brief summary (56, 57) of what he later expands in Romans, showing not only that death has been overcome by resurrection but also that those enemies that brought death – sin and the law – are also doomed. He sees sin as the deadly poison that has led to death, and the law as that which gives sin its power (see Romans 7). In itself the law is 'good' (Romans 7:13), but it leads to proud self-righteousness in those who think they obey it. It also exposes and even aggravates human depravity and rebellion against God.

Christ's victory over death is evidence that he has overcome both the sin that caused death (in this sense, death is not something 'natural') and the law that empowers sin. So, in a final shout of praise, Paul rejoices in that present victory which God has given his people in the cross, by which sin and the law have already been defeated. Once again, Christ ('our Lord Jesus Christ') is seen as the one through whom God has effected all this.

The basis or motivation which Paul gives for all that he has said in this chapter is that believers do not labour in vain (2, 4, 17). So with a

187

humility that recognizes that the victory is in Christ, and not in ourselves, we can nevertheless sing the taunt of death even now, in the light of Christ's resurrection. The death that could not hold Jesus (*cf.* Acts 2:24) will not be able to hold us either, and even now we have the foretaste of this in victory over sin and law. So although in one sense this chapter might move us to 'look into the sky' (Acts 1:11), properly understood, it impels us to get on with our work!

Questions
1. What kind of body will we have when we finally rise with Christ? (It would be good to list as many of those things as possible that can be said about it.)
2. Carefully apply verse 58 to the life of your group or church. What does God say to you through this verse?
3. The world is full of pain, injustice and premature death. What kept Paul's faith alive? What about yours?

14

THE LAST
WORD
1 Corinthians 16:1–24

1 Corinthians 16:1–12

Back in the valley

Glory may be coming, but in the meantime we have to get down to the hard work of disciplined and costly discipleship.

 Paul has shown those Corinthians who thought that they were already in the 'heavenlies' that the final condition of every true believer is still future. Meanwhile *labour in the Lord* is the order of the day (15:58)!

Advice on giving

With this in mind he turns to another question raised by the Corinthians' letter (compare, for example, 7:1): the collection for the church in Jerusalem (1: see Romans 15:25–27). In view of the selfish and inward-looking attitudes of many within the Corinthian church it is significant that Paul reminds them of their fellowship with and obligations to Christians elsewhere. Paul had worked out the most effective way to make the collection, having already shared his detailed plan with the Galatian churches (1).

His advice is practical and very down to earth (2). Regularly, every one of the believers in the church was to set aside something for the collection (possibly the first day of the week is mentioned because it was becoming the usual day for Christians to gather together).

With pastoral realism, Paul does not set any specific targets. He suggests, however, that giving should be proportionate to the amount with which God had prospered them during the previous week. Since some of the members of the church were slaves, this was a wise strategy. It would also ensure that a sudden 'whip-round' was not required when he arrived in the city.

This procedure was likely to raise an amount that would justify a delegation being sent to Jerusalem with it. The delegation would be sent with the appropriate paperwork that was required in the business world of Paul's time (3, 4).

The apostle adds that, if it can be made to fit in with his plans, he might join the delegation. On other occasions he might receive supernatural guidance. Here, however, it is implied that decision-making is usually far more down to earth.

Making decisions

Verses 5–9 give details of Paul's travel plans (see map on p. 12). The apostle was writing from Ephesus, where he intended to stay a little longer. The reference to Pentecost suggests that this letter was, therefore, written in the spring, probably of AD 55.

Paul did not then intend to take the direct route to Corinth across the Aegean Sea, the route this letter would presumably be taking. The shipping season usually resumed on 5 March after a winter break. Rather, he was determined to visit Macedonia. Probably it would be autumn by the time he arrived in Corinth and this would enable him to spend the winter there with the church.

Such were his plans, but they were always subject to the Lord's will. In fact (as more detailed studies show) various changes were subsequently made and altered before Paul eventually arrived at Corinth.

Paul's reference to the situation in Ephesus almost certainly ties in with the events recorded in Acts 19; opportunities for the gospel frequently go hand in hand with opposition and difficulty. Paul's response indicates that he did not see difficulty as evidence that he was out of God's will. Some people at Corinth did believe this and many are tempted to believe it still. But God never promises his servants an easy ride. Problems are not necessarily a sign that we have missed God's way.

Apollos and Timothy commended

Meanwhile Timothy, probably with several assistants (11), had already gone on to Macedonia and might be planning to visit Corinth. Paul no longer knew their detailed plans as they were too far away, but he may have suggested that Timothy visit Corinth as his authorized representative (4:17).

Timothy might be unwelcome at Corinth as a representative of the unpopular Paul. Sensitive perhaps to Timothy's timidity (if this is implied in, for example, 1 Timothy 1:3; 4:12), Paul reminds the fellowship that Timothy is about the Lord's work and deserves their support. With a touch of irony, perhaps, the apostle reminds them that he, too, is serving the Lord! His hopes for the fellowship he loved (see, for example, verse 24) were that Timothy might be accepted and sent back to Paul having enjoyed full and unspoilt fellowship with the Corinthians (see 'What happened next?' p. 193).

The 'Now about' (12) suggests that Paul is referring to a request in the Corinthians' letter to him that Apollos be encouraged to visit their church. This request might well have come from the 'Apollos party' (see 1:12). It is noteworthy, therefore, that Paul refers to him as a brother and had urged Apollos to accept. It is significant that Apollos said no. Indeed, it is possible that 'opportunity' implies 'when you have made it right for him to come'. All this emphasizes that the two men were not themselves opposed to one another and were each acting in a manner which sought to encourage and protect the other. What 'big men' these early church leaders were!

Questions
1. What lessons can I learn from this passage to guide my giving?
2. How does this passage help us to find God's will for us?
3. Does your congregation look first to its own needs or outwards to the needs of the world when it discusses finances?
4. The early church was both international and interdependent. How does the present passage demonstrate this and challenge current church attitudes?

The collection

In New Testament times Jerusalem was not a wealthy city and there was widespread poverty among its inhabitants. The Jewish community outside Palestine, therefore, frequently sent gifts for distribution among the poor of the city.

The Jerusalem church was not exempt from these problems (Acts 6:1–6) and the so-called experiment in primitive communism (Acts 2:44, 45; 4:32) may, in the longer term, have made things worse when capital resources ran out. It is also likely that, as Christians became distinguished from Jews, the church would have ceased to receive the handouts from which they had previously benefited. In such circumstances the famine of AD 46 must must have been a severe blow and prompted action by the wider Christian community (Acts 11:28). The problem did not, however, go away, and so (sometime during his third missionary journey) Paul resolved that the present collection was needed. This passage indicates that the Corinthians were already familiar with Paul's idea and had sought more information.

The New Testament writings only hint at Paul's motives. Clearly the existence of the need was itself probably the primary reason for the collection. But there may have been other reasons; it might help to cement relations between the Jewish and non-Jewish Christian communities and it might well be important to show that the Christian communities outside Palestine looked after their Palestinian brothers and sisters as well as did the Jewish community. Whatever Paul's reasons (and compare Romans 15:25–27 for a more theological reason), he clearly believed that there was strong obligation resting on the churches to meet the need.

2 Corinthians 8 and 9 give a full discussion of Paul's views on the subject.

What happened next?

We do not know whether Timothy actually visited Corinth as planned, or how such a visit turned out if he did get there! However, it does appear that soon afterwards Paul changed his plans and made a short, unexpected visit to Corinth (2 Corinthians 2:1–4). This may have been occasioned by Timothy's report.

Paul's visit appears to have been a disaster, and for the time being he was unwilling to return. Titus (not Timothy) was then sent to the church (2 Corinthians 2:13; 7:6–7).

1 Corinthians 16:13–24
Summing up

In concluding his letter, Paul sets out the challenges we must face if we are to follow Jesus faithfully.

 Very briefly and in the light of all that he has said, Paul puts down a fivefold challenge to the Corinthian church (13). Using language borrowed from the military, he stresses the urgent need to be ever vigilant against perversions of the gospel and to hold fast to the apostolic teaching. This demands courage, since the battle may be fierce and costly.

But motive is of supreme importance, so Paul adds that such actions must be done graciously and with sympathetic concern for the person holding to, or teetering on the edge of, error (14).

Once again, Paul's wisdom shines through. How easy to slip from love into dangerous sentimentality if the truth is abandoned! How easy to become coldly critical where love is forgotten! But error is not resolved by capitulation and the battle is not won without love. The different groups in Corinth seemed to have forgotten this.

Greetings to old friends

But not all of them have forgotten (15–18)! Together with Fortunatus and Achaicus, Stephanus, an old friend of Paul, apparently had been sent from the church with the letter Paul is now answering. And Stephanus was a living example of the sort of lifestyle that Paul desired all the Corinthian church to follow. He and his household were devoted ('addicted' is implied!) to the service of others. There is no suggestion that this had followed some sort of appointment to ministry. Rather it was something they had done entirely of 'themselves'. There were others too; and Paul's wish is that everyone

194

else should follow their example of loving care for others.

It is not surprising that the apostle found refreshment in fellowship with such people (nor were the Corinthian church strangers to the blessing of having such people among them!). Equally unsurprising (or is it?) is Paul's commendation of them. Only such people deserve recognition in the church. Perhaps the implication here is that they had not, however, received it.

Final farewell

The greetings offered here (19–22) are typical of many a first-century letter. Yet the comprehensive list here seems to be intended to jolt the Corinthian church out of their selfish, independent spirit. They were part of an international fellowship of brothers and sisters who loved them and were interested deeply in their welfare.

They also needed to be reminded that they themselves were a family (20b). The family kiss, seriously undertaken, was a pledge of love and forgiveness. No church ever needed to recall the significance of this custom more than strife-torn Corinth.

Signing off

It was customary in ancient times for letters to be written by a secretary and for the author to sign it. Paul, however, cannot end with a mere signature. Picking up the pen and filled with the deepest emotion, he adds a couple of sentences. Briefly, he says three things:

- Failure to live in love as a fellowship (the mark of true love for the Lord) indicates that the curse of God rests on them. *Come, O Lord,* or 'Maranatha', is Palestinian Aramaic (presumably in the same way as we use 'Amen' or 'Hallelujah', it was familiar to them). Paul's point appears to be this: 'Remember the confession you make in the fellowship. It is true. But are you ready for his coming or must he come to curse you?' It is difficult to imagine a more serious challenge to true Christian discipleship!

- His wish is that they all enjoy the grace of God. This is a pointed comment when we recall that the Corinthians thought in terms of specially privileged groups within the church. They needed to be reminded that the gospel is a good news of grace which is freely available to all who seek it.

- Finally, Paul assures his readers of his love for all of them because of the Saviour they shared. It had been a difficult letter to write but the motive for it had been love. After all, love is ready to pay the price for speaking the truth. The challenge the Corinthians had to face was whether they were big enough to receive Paul's loving rebuke!

Questions
1. What challenges does this passage offer to my own life of disciple-ship?
2. What effect might a kiss of peace, thoughtfully undertaken, have in your church?
3. If the church is a worldwide community, how can we make this a reality?
4. What are the main lessons that we have learned from our study of 1 Corinthians? Would Paul be surprised at our answer to the question?

(If you are working in a group you might like to make the last question the subject of a whole meeting.)

For further reading

One commentary stands head and shoulders above all the rest: Gordon D. Fee, *The First Epistle to the Corinthians* (Eerdmans, 1987). Written by the foremost Pentecostal New Testament scholar in the world, it supersedes most of the earlier scholarly or semi-scholarly works.

An interesting supplement to Fee is David Prior, *The Message of 1 Corinthians*, The Bible Speaks Today series (IVP, 1985). This is not really a commentary but the author's application to today of the book's message. Written by an Anglican associated with the renewal movement, it offers some interesting and fresh perspectives on 1 Corinthians.

The authors of this Bible Guide stand within neither of these traditions but have found that these two volumes have usually offered the clearest explanation and application of 1 Corinthians available. It goes without saying that we have not always agreed with them or followed their lead!

Also helpful are Leon Morris, *1 Corinthians*, Tyndale New Testament Commentary (IVP, 1985) and D. A. Carson, *The Cross and Christian Ministry: An Exposition of Passages from 1 Corinthians* (IVP, 1993).

For a concise overview see Bruce Winter, '1 Corinthians', in the *New Bible Commentary*, 21st-century edition (IVP, 1994).

Robin Dowling teaches the Bible and pastoral studies at the Biblical Seminary of Colombia in Medellín. Before going to the mission field in 1992, he was a Baptist pastor for fifteen years in Kew. His B.S. degree is from Bath University, and he has studied at Spurgeon's College.

Stephen Dray teaches biblical interpretation and preaching at Moorlands College in Bournemouth. Before joining the Moorlands faculty in 1988, he was a Baptist pastor for ten years in London. His B.D. degree is from London Bible College. He now edits the journal *Evangel*.